The Egyptian Bureaucracy

Modern Arab Studies
Tareq Y. Ismael, Series Editor

The Egyptian Bureaucracy

Monte Palmer

Ali Leila

El Sayed Yassin

SYRACUSE UNIVERSITY PRESS

First Edition
First published 1988
98 97 96 95 94 93 92 91 90 89 88   5 4 3 2 1

MONTE PALMER is Professor of Political Science, Florida State University, and the author of *Dilemmas of Political Development*. EL SAYED YASSIN is Director of the Al Ahram Center for Political and Strategic Studies in Egypt and the author of *Rich States and Poor States in the Middle East*. ALI LEILA is Professor of Sociology at Ein Shams University in Cairo.

The paper used in this publication meets the minimum requirements of American National Standard for Information Services—Permanence of Paper for Printed Library Materials, ANSI Z39.48-1984.∞™

Library of Congress Cataloging-in-Publication Data

Palmer, Monte.
    The Egyptian bureaucracy/Monte Palmer, Ali
    Leila.—1st ed.
        p.   cm.—(Modern Arab studies)
    Bibliography: p.
    Includes index.
    ISBN 0-8156-2455-7 (alk. paper)
    1. Bureaucracy—Egypt. 2. Egypt—Politics
and government—1981–   . 3. Economic
development projects—Political aspects—Egypt.
4. Community development—Political aspects—
Egypt. I. Leila, Ali. II. Title. III. Series.
JQ3831.P35   1988
354.6201—dc19   88-20063
                                       CIP

Manufactured in the United States of America

Contents

	Tables	vii
	Preface	ix
1	Bureaucracy in Egypt: An Overview	1
2	The Bureaucratic Milieu	19
3	Apathy, Values, Incentives, and Development	45
4	Bureaucratic Flexibility and Development in Egypt	73
5	Innovation and Bureaucracy in Egypt	91
6	Bureaucracy and the Public	107
7	The Attributes of Bureaucratic Performance	121
8	Summary, Conclusions, and Recommendations	147
	Notes	165
	Bibliography	173
	Index	183

Tables

2.1.	Advantages of a Bureaucratic Career	39
2.2.	Method of Recruitment	40
3.1.	Assessments of Low Productivity among Egyptian Bureaucrats by Senior Officials	49
3.2.	Group Dynamics Scale	50
3.3.	Measures of Bureaucratic Productivity	51
3.4.	Job Satisfaction and Dissatisfaction	52
3.5.	Some Explanations of Low Productivity among Egyptian Bureaucrats by Senior Officials	60
3.6.	Senior-Level Perceptions of the Main Problems Reducing the Administrative Effectiveness of the Egyptian Bureaucracy	63
3.7.	Main Incentive Values of Egyptian Bureaucrats	66
4.1.	Centralization of Decision Making (Senior Officials Only)	79
4.2.	Some Explanations of Centralization (Senior Bureaucrats Only)	81
4.3.	Responsibility Avoidance among Egyptian Bureaucrats	85
4.4.	Vertical Communications	87
4.6.	Horizontal Communications	88
5.1.	Assessments of Bureaucratic Innovation	93
5.2.	Predispositions toward Social innovation	94
5.3.	Innovation in Decision Making	96
5.4.	Explanations of Low Bureaucratic Innovation	103

6.1. Self-Perceptions of Bureaucratic Social Status   112
6.2. Bureaucratic Perceptions of the Egyptian Public   113
6.3. Bureaucratic Explanations of Conflict between the
     Bureaucracy and the Public   116
6.4. Who Is to Blame?   119
7.1. Media Habits of Egyptian Bureaucrats   134
7.2. Information Reference Sources   139
7.3. Positive Reinforcement   141
7.4. Systemic Influences on Bureaucratic Behavior   143

Preface

The Egyptian bureaucracy has long been the object of criticism within the Egyptian media. In recent years, however, concern over the performance of the Egyptian bureaucracy has gone beyond journalistic criticism. It is now apparent that the Egyptian bureaucracy is a major obstacle to the economic and social development of Egyptian society.

Addressing this reality, the Al Ahram Center for Political and Strategic Studies initiated a major study of the Egyptian bureaucracy in the fall of 1983. The project, supported by the Ford Foundation, was designed to provide an empirical assessment of the capacity of the Egyptian bureaucracy to play a forceful role in Egypt's economic and social development during the coming decade. Building upon excellent historical and organizational studies of the Egyptian bureaucracy by Ayubi, Youssef, and others, the Al Ahram study placed particular emphasis on the behavioral dimensions of the bureaucratic peformance. Why, to paraphrase President Mubarak, didn't Egyptian bureaucrats work as hard as they should? And how could this situation be redressed?

Within this context, the Al Ahram project (1) assessed the extent to which behavior patterns said to be inimical to the developmental capacity of the Egyptian bureaucracy were indeed present within the bureaucracy, (2) examined diverse explanations for the existence of such behavior patterns, and (3) suggested ways in which behavior patterns likely to improve the developmental capacity of the Egyptian bureaucracy could be enhanced.

The data presented in the ensuing pages are based upon a survey of 836 Egyptian civil servants conducted by the Al Ahram Center for

Strategic and Political Studies during the late spring of 1983. The sample was selected in relatively equal proportions from three government sector agencies: the Ministry of Social Affairs, the Ministry of Industry, and the Aluminum Corporation. Collectively, the three administrative agencies represent (1) a service-oriented bureaucracy, (2) a production-oriented bureaucracy, and (3) an on-line public sector bureaucracy. The Aluminum Corporation was selected because of its reputation as one of the most productive of Egypt's public sector companies, thereby providing an opportunity to examine the bureaucratic process in what is reputed to be one of Egypt's best-run bureaucracies.

The Al Ahram study also drew upon a wide variety of government reports, Ph.D. dissertations, press reports, and personal interviews. We would also be less than candid if we did not acknowledge the experience and participant observation of members of the research team.

The project was headed by El Sayeed Yassin, the director of the Center. Members of the research team included Ali Leila of Ein Shams University, Monte Palmer of Florida State University and a Senior Research Fellow of the Center, and Olfat Aga of the Al Ahram Center. The members of the research team wish to express their appreciation to all the officials that participated in the survey. Particular appreciation is also due to the Minister of Social Affairs, the Minister of Industry, and the Director of the Aluminum Corporation. Special thanks are also due to Mr. Mustafa Al Khouri of the Al Ahram Computing Center for his willingness to work long and irregular hours in order to expedite the timely completion of the project. We would also like to express our deepest appreciation to the Ford Foundation and to Dr. Ann Lesch, the program officer in charge of the Al Ahram project. Thanks, too, is due Sayeed al Majid, Kathie Austin, and Mary Schneider for their invaluable assistance to various stages of the project.

All errors and omissions in the execution of the project and in the preparation of this volume remain the sole responsibility of the authors. The opinions expressed in this volume are the authors' and do not reflect the official views of the Ford Foundation or the Al Ahram Center.

1

ℐℬ

Bureaucracy in Egypt

An Overview

The Egyptian bureaucracy, in common with most bureaucracies of the Third World, performs two basic functions. First, it maintains an ever-increasing array of services essential to the day-to-day operation of the state. Secondly, it bears primary responsibility for the economic and social development of Egyptian society. Both functions are critical to the political and economic viability of the Egyptian state. If the bureaucracy falters in its ability to deliver an adequate level of maintenance services, the Egyptian government may soon find it impossible to cope with the demands of a burgeoning population that is expected to double within the next twenty years. By the same token, if the bureaucracy cannot or will not play a dynamic role in the areas of economic and social development, the economic shortages and social dislocations of the present era will merely be exacerbated, presenting future generations with economic and social problems of incalculable proportions.

What, then, is the capacity of the Egyptian bureaucracy to provide the citizens of Egypt with an adequate level of services? And, in particular, what is the capacity of the Egyptian bureaucracy to play a dynamic role in the economic and social development of Egyptian society?

In an effort to provide answers to these questions, the Al Ahram Center for Strategic and Political Studies undertook a major analysis of the developmental capacity of the Egyptian bureaucracy. The Al Ahram study was supported by a grant from the Ford Foundation and centered on a sample survey of bureaucratic attitudes and behavior. In addition to the survey, the study included informal interviews with a variety of administrators, politicians, and scholars.

The results of the Al Ahram study are presented in three sections. The initial section, chapters 1 and 2, provides a general overview of the Egyptian bureaucracy and outlines the critical role that the bureaucracy must play in the developmental process. The initial section also examines the social and political milieus in which the Egyptian bureaucracy operates as well as the massive economic and social problems for which it must find solutions if Egypt is to enter the final decade of the twentieth century with a reasonable hope of achieving sustained economic growth. The second section of the volume, chapters 3 through 7, presents the results of the survey of 826 Egyptian civil servants that constituted the central focus of the Al Ahram project. These chapters assess the developmental capacity of the Egyptian bureaucracy and explore some of the reasons for its lackluster performance during the past decades. The third section of the volume, chapter 8, summarizes the results of the Al Ahram study and presents recommendations for bureaucratic reform based upon the data presented in chapters 1 through 7.

Bureaucracy and Development under Nasser and Sadat

In the years that have elapsed since Egypt attained independence from the British in 1923, successive Egyptian governments have struggled with the problems of overpopulation, poverty, illiteracy, social inequality, and underdevelopment. The efforts of postrevolutionary governments to alleviate these problems achieved major successes in the areas of health, education, social justice, and human services. Indeed, Egypt now exports its administrative and educational expertise to most of the oil-producing states of the region. In spite of successes in the areas of health and education, however, Egypt's own economic and social development has been slow and halting. Illiteracy continues to be a problem, the economy is lethargic, and rampant population growth threatens to erode the economic and social gains of the past decades.

Egypt's disappointing record in the areas of social and economic development during the first half of the twentieth century can be attributed to a variety of factors. Until 1923, Egypt languished under various forms and degrees of colonial domination. Economic progress during the years of the monarchy was depressed by political conflicts, by an over-dependence upon primary exports (cotton), by the lack of a strong domestic market, by the mercantile policies of the British, by the dislocations of two world wars, by a rampant population explosion, and by the presence of a political regime that was either unwilling or unable to provide concerted leadership in the fields of economic and social development. The Egyptian bureaucracy, for its part, was ill equipped to plan, stimulate, or otherwise play a major role in the development of the Egyptian economy. Indeed, as Egypt moved deeper into the Farouk era, the Egyptian bureaucracy was used primarily to maintain order and to feed Farouk's insatiable demands for revenue. The economy, largely in the hands of foreigners, was allowed to shift for itself.[1]

The July revolution of 1952 was a product of the monarchy's inability to address Egypt's burgeoning social and economic problems. The revolution's foremost goals were the economic and social development of Egypt and the redressing of centuries of social inequality. The randomness of laissez-faire economics was replaced by centralized economic planning and by concerted efforts to redistribute Egypt's wealth on a just and equitable basis that would provide all Egyptians with at least minimal levels of health, education, housing, and employment. The key words of the era were development and human dignity. Just how these goals were to be achieved was to be worked out with time.[2]

The leaders of the 1952 revolution placed almost total responsibility for the planning and the implementation of their massive economic and social development programs upon the shoulders of the Egyptian bureaucracy. This became even more the case with the nationalization of foreign banks, insurance companies, and industrial organizations in the aftermath of the tripartite aggression of 1956, and the subsequent nationalization of all major economic and commercial establishments in 1961.[3] Indeed, with the advent of the socialist laws of 1961, the ability of the revolutionary government to develop Egypt economically and socially would depend almost entirely upon the capacity of the Egyptian bureaucracy to innovate, plan, coordinate, produce, distribute, and apply economic and social programs on a scale seldom found beyond the confines of the socialist bloc. The success or failure of Egypt's economic and social development would henceforth be the success or failure of the Egyptian bureaucracy.

The burdens of social and economic development, however, were not the only burdens to be placed upon the shoulders of the Egyptian bureaucracy during the Nasser era. Nasser demanded a bureaucracy that embraced socialism as its ideology, a bureaucracy that would impose that ideology upon the masses. The burdens placed upon the frail structure of the bureaucracy, then, were complex indeed.

The bureaucracy inherited from the monarchy was clearly inadequate to the challenges of the revolutionary era. Its numbers were small, its structure was oriented toward control rather than development, and its leadership was tainted by its royal origins. Moreover, it was not at all clear in the minds of Egypt's revolutionary leaders that those who had served the king could also serve the revolution. Reflecting this concern, one of the early acts of the revolutionary government was the establishment of "purge committees" charged with the task of ensuring loyalty, integrity, productivity, and efficiency in government.[4] One source suggests that approximately one-half of the senior officials of Farouk's bureaucracy fell victim to the purge committees.[5]

Reflecting its new and diverse responsibilities, the Egyptian bureaucracy would swell from 250,000 employees in 1952 to approximately 1,200,000 by 1970. The number of ministries would increase from fifteen to twenty-eight during the same period. Public corporations, an artifact of the nationalization of foreign firms and the socialist laws, would jump from one in 1957, the first year of the expropriations, to thirty-eight in 1963. By 1970 their number would reach forty-six.[6]

Bureaucratic expansion, however, was not motivated solely by the staffing requirements of the bureaucracy and the newly acquired public sector. Bureaucratic growth was also spurred by a conscious decision to use government service as a means of reducing intellectual unemployment among the thousands of graduates emerging from the revolution's expanded education system. Under the newly proclaimed "graduates policy," university students were guaranteed bureaucratic positions upon graduation.

Superficially, at least, the graduates policy appeared compatible with the rapid expansion of bureaucratic functions initiated by the revolution. The bureaucracy was in short supply of talent; the graduates, presumably the cream of Egyptian society, needed jobs. Things, however, were not as they seemed. The urgency of the moment precluded the rational allocation of personnel on the basis of need or qualifications. Jobs had to be done. Programs had to be put into operation. If existing organizations faltered, new units had to be created. Functions overlapped and jurisdictions merged. Laws and regulations proliferated. The skills of the new graduates were not well suited to the demands of the moment either. Most had specialized in the arts, law, or the humanities. Their lack of practical skills was exceeded only by their expectations of authority.[7] As years passed, the number of graduates demanding government employment would far exceed the needs of the bureaucracy. By the early 1980s, many graduates would be forced to wait from two to four years for their promised bureaucratic positions.

The revolutionary government was not unaware of its bureaucratic problems. The shortcomings of the bureaucracy were discussed openly in the press. The calls for reform were many. The problems, however, would be sorted out once the dust had settled and the new programs were in place. Revolutions, after all, are not orderly affairs. In the short run, the regime would rely on the military to provide the bureaucracy with the force and the discipline necessary to accomplish their tasks. Twenty-five percent of the corporate managers in the public sector during the 1960s, for example, were seconded from the military.[8] Top bureaucratic officials were also shifted from unit to unit in an effort to increase productivity. The Nasser regime, then, pursued its economic development and social equality programs with revolutionary zeal. Administrative problems, while many, would work themselves out in the course of time. Time, however, would always be of the essence. Two decades of conflict with Israel, a disastrous military involvement in Yemen, and the heady pursuit of Arab unity preempted the energies of the Nasser regime and precluded a comprehensive reform of the bureaucracy.

The Nasser era, in sum, transformed Egypt into a bureaucratic state. Few areas of political, economic, or social life in Egypt were to be free from government involvement in one form or another. The Egyptian bureaucracy swelled to meet the needs of the new era, yet its structure and organization were poorly suited to the task. Also problematic were the attitudes and behavior patterns of many Egyptian bureaucrats. The revolution may have inspired zeal and optimism among its political leaders, but it did little to shake the lethargy and complacency of its civil servants.[9]

The transition from Abdul Nasser to Anwar Sadat in 1970

dramatically redefined the policy orientations of the Egyptian government. State socialism would be tempered by the revitalization of the Egyptian private sector under Sadat's *infitah* or open-door policy. The Arab Socialist Union would give way to an abortive experiment with multiparty politics. Nasserites and elements of the political left, once the dominant force in Egyptian politics, would find themselves outflanked by Sadat's nurturing of the Islamic right. The Soviet Union, Egypt's stalwart ally during a decade and a half of conflict with Israel, would give way to an Egyptian-American axis founded on the normalization of Egyptian-Israeli relations and the dismantling of Nasser's pan-Arab policies.

The dramatic shifts in public and foreign policy initiated by the Sadat regime did little to enhance the circumstances of the Egyptian bureaucracy. Socialism continued to be a key element in the ideology of the state. The revolution's infrastructure of state planning, price supports, and public corporations would remain the dominant elements in Egypt's economic superstructure. The private sector, aside from agriculture, tended to concentrate its efforts in the lucrative areas of banking, real estate, construction, and tourism. Economic development, in spite of the optimistic expectations of Sadat's *infitah,* continued to be linked directly to the developmental capacity of the Egyptian bureaucracy. The developmental promise of *infitah* simply did not materialize. [10]

Egypt's bureaucratic problems were also not eased by Sadat's shift of allegiance from the Soviet Union to the United States. While the United States committed itself to provide Egypt with some $5 billion in various forms of aid in the years between 1975 and 1980, the Egyptians and the Americans were soon to find themselves at loggerheads over the strategies, projects, and ideology embodied in the AID program. [11] By the late 1970s, a massive USAID bureaucracy was well entrenched in Cairo, its primary functions being to plan and implement projects that were (1) desired by the Egyptians, (2) judged feasible by American experts, (3) compatible with Egypt's needs, plans, and priorities, and (4) met the ideological and bureaucratic conditions imposed by Washington. Washington's bureaucratic conditions, among other things, included multiple ministerial clearances and fiscal accountability regulations. While not unreasonable from the American perspective, such clearances and regulations were judged cumbersome if not insulting by the Egyptians. Israel, as the Egyptians were wont to point out, received lump-sum grants from the United States that involved none of the red tape of the American aid program to Egypt. Why shouldn't Egypt also receive lump-sum grants and pursue its own economic development unfettered by U.S. interference? Aid agreements also required that most of the USAID dollars received by Egypt be spent in the United States, use U.S. shipping, and employ U.S. firms. Again, while such legislation appeared eminently reasonable from the American perspective, it was perceived as unduly costly, time consuming, and complex by the Egyptians. In many cases, goods and services could be purchased far more cheaply on the world market than they could in the United States.

Perhaps more damning from the Egyptian perspective was the ideological conflict that was to develop between USAID and the Egyptian planners. The heart of the conflict centered on the role of the private sector in Egypt's economic development. The Egyptian economy, as noted above, is dominated by the public sector. Even after a decade of *infitah,* approximately 70 percent of the manufacturing sector remains in the public sector. With the advent of the Reagan era, the United States began to use the leverage of its aid programs to force the development of the Egyptian private sector. More zealous elements in the USAID hierarchy would have preferred to see the total dismantling of the public sector and the full return of Egypt to a private economy. This view, needless to say, stood in sharp contradiction to Egypt's revolutionary values of social justice and public ownership. It also posed a threat to a bureaucratic elite deeply entrenched within the government ministries and the state industrial organizations.

Conflicts over ideology also extended to the area of developmental strategy. Egyptian planners and bureaucrats perceived the enlargement and modernization of the government-owned heavy industries such as steel and aluminum as the optimal means for maximizing both economic development and mass employment. The American position, by contrast, favored the diversification of aid monies into a variety of light industrial projects more in keeping with Egypt's capacities and needs. Light industries were also more compatible with an expansion of the private sector. Egypt's public corporations, in the American view, were cumbersome and inefficient. The American position was recently expressed by Frank Kimball, the current director of USAID in Egypt.

> I think there is a much larger role the private sector could play. Currently, the private sector in Egypt is largely in trade, services

and construction. They could play a bigger role by becoming more involved in manufacturing and technology transfer. The big challenge for the private sector and for Egypt is to create meaningful employment for the 300,000 to 400,000 people who enter the job market each year. . . .

Today we don't have an awful lot of U.S. (private) investment here, only about $60 million. We're trying to encourage them, but it's a slow process. Also, the government needs to work on a number of problems, not the least of which is making the bureaucracy more responsive. . . .

They have a lot of work to do with the bureaucracy. The government is overblown. There is way too much public employment. . . . I think state-run industries are a drain on the budget.[12]

The impact of American aid on the Egyptian bureaucracy was threefold. First, new organizational mechanisms had to be created to interface with a massive USAID bureaucracy encamped in Cairo. Second, both the public sector organizations and the mainline bureaucracy were being forced into a defensive posture. Their previous position of invulnerability was clearly being challenged. Third, the myriad pressures and constraints tied to the U.S. aid program added yet another dimension of complexity and uncertainty to what was already a ponderous bureaucratic process.

The Sadat regime, in spite of its private sector initiative, witnessed a dramatic increase in the size of the Egyptian bureaucracy. By 1978, 1,900,000 Egyptians were employed by the Egyptian government, excluding employees in the public sector companies. When the latter are added, the figure jumps to approximately 3,200,000.[13] To these figures must be added the approximately 100,000 university graduates petitioning annually for positions in the bureaucracy.

The key legacy of the Sadat era in terms of bureaucratic capacity, however, was not the growth of an already unwieldy apparatus. It was the demoralization of the bureaucracy. Sadat's newly revitalized private sector created a new economic class receiving wages several times higher than the corresponding wages received by government employees. A typical Egyptian teacher, to put the situation in perspective, receives the equivalent of approximately $40 per month. The lowest rung on the government pay scale is a meager $20 per month.[14] A taxi driver, with luck, can earn several times that amount in a single week. Under the Nasser regime, the economic rules, with some exceptions, were more or less equal for everyone. Salaries were low and there were few luxury goods to purchase with the monies received. Rent controls and subsidized food compensated for the low wages and ensured government employees a minimally adequate standard of living. Under Sadat's open door policy, by contrast, the Egyptian market was flooded with luxury items, most of which were well beyond the reach of the average government employee. Many government employees with marketable skills either deserted government service for the private sector or accepted extremely lucrative positions in the Gulf. No less than one-third of the respondents in the Al Ahram survey, by way of illustration, were primed to seek positions in either the private sector or the Gulf. Yet another one-third were weighing the possibilities of such a move. Moreover, the percentage of males willing to seek work in the Gulf or the private sector was substantially higher when the data was controlled for sex.

In retrospect, then, the Sadat era witnessed the growth of the Egyptian bureaucracy in both size and complexity. It also witnessed the demoralization of the bureaucracy and the flight of many of its most skilled and experienced members to the private sector or the Gulf. Rather than solving the bureaucratic problems of the Nasser era, the Sadat regime merely compounded them.

Anwar Sadat, it must be noted, was not unaware of Egypt's bureaucratic problems. Sporadic attempts to reform the bureaucracy had been initiated as early as 1974, but they went largely for naught. In his Labor Day speech of 1977, however, Sadat demanded an "administrative revolution," a revolution that would destroy routine and red tape and safeguard the public interest.[15]

Sadat's call for an administrative revolution was widely heralded in the Egyptian press and sparked a national debate on the best way to reform the bureaucracy. As with earlier calls for reform, however, Sadat's administrative revolution turned out to be little more than a media event. Less than a year after its inauguration, the weekly news magazine *Rose Al Yousif* referred to the administrative revolution as "slogan without substance and noise without action," adding that "despite all this noise, published articles, seminars and reports, nothing materialized. The general administrative nature is still characterized by carelessness and irresponsibility. Most of the government units house groups of human beings working under difficult financial and moral conditions. In such conditions, it is almost impossible to increase productivity or the quality of production."[16]

Similar caustic comments were echoed by all of the major Cairo papers. *Al Ahrar* mockingly referred to the administrative revolution as an annual event.[17] *Al Ahram* was even more critical, condemning coverage of the administrative revolution on radio and television as a "joke," and asking "How can we achieve an administrative revolution while top people still think that nothing went wrong . . . and those people who created the problem are still in charge."[18]

The Bureaucratic Challenge in the Mubarak Era

When Hosni Mubarak assumed the presidency of Egypt in 1981, he inherited a staggering array of social, economic, and political problems. His ability to solve these problems depends, as it did in the eras of Nasser and Sadat, upon the developmental capacity of the Egyptian bureaucracy.

The Al Ahram project, as noted in the introductory comments, was initiated to assess the capacity of the Egyptian bureaucracy to play a dynamic role in meeting the challenges confronting Egypt as it prepares to enter the final decade of the twentieth century and to suggest ways in which that capacity might be improved. Four steps are required to place the results and recommendations of the Al Ahram study in perspective. First, it is necessary to examine the challenges that confront the Egyptian bureaucracy. It is difficult to assess the capacity of the Egyptian bureaucracy without at least a basic notion of the task at hand. Second, it is necessary to provide a standard for assessing the capacity of the Egyptian bureaucracy. What attributes must the Egyptian bureaucracy possess if it is to play a dynamic role in the developmental process? Third, in order to benefit from the efforts of prior research and to gain a broader understanding of the problems of the Egyptian bureaucracy, it is necessary to provide an overview of that bureaucracy based upon the existing literature. What are the prevailing views of the Egyptian bureaucracy and its developmental capacity? Finally, an assessment of the developmental capacity of the Egyptian bureaucracy requires at least a rudimentary understanding of the political, social, and economic milieus in which the bureaucracy operates. Bureaucracies do not operate in a vacuum and they cannot be reformed in a vacuum. The remainder of the present chapter will outline the major challenges confronting the Egyptian bureaucracy during the Mubarak era. Chapter 2, in turn, will examine the problems of assessing the bureaucratic capacity in Egypt and will place the bureaucracy in its economic, political, and cultural milieus. Chapter 2 will also review relevant methodological data relating to the Al Ahram project.

Heading the many challenges confronting the Mubarak regime is Egypt's population explosion. Egypt's population in 1960 was approximately 20 million. By 1980, the figure exceeded 40 million. It threatens to top the 70 million mark by the turn of the century, barring the initiation of dramatic and severe birth-control measures.[19] Coupled with staggering population growth is Egypt's dependence upon foreign assistance to feed its present population of 44 million. Annual consumption of wheat increased from 2 million tons in 1960 to 7 million tons in 1980 and a projected 8.6 million tons in 1985. Requirements for corn have similarly risen from 1.6 million tons in 1960 to 4.2 million tons in 1980 and a projected 5.2 million tons in 1985.[20]

If Egypt's requirements for food have increased in proportion to increases in population, food production has not. Areas of cultivatable land have remained static. Even more problematic is the apparent decrease in the cultivation of basic food crops resulting from the high cost of agrarian labor in relation to the price controls imposed by the government. Farmers, in effect, are forced to absorb at least some of the costs of government subsidies on basic foods. Reflecting the infinite complexity of economic and bureaucratic life in Egypt, President Sadat's economic liberalization policies, the *infitah,* made it far more lucrative for Egypt's *fellahin* to seek their fortune in the oil states or to migrate to Egypt's commercial centers than to remain in the fields at a subsistence wage. Pricing caps on agrarian products, however, were retained as part of government price supports and as a hedge against the inflationary impact of the *infitah*. To have abolished price supports and allowed agrarian products to seek their market value—a policy urged upon Egypt by the United States and the International Monetary Fund—would have increased local food production. It would also have shattered government wage structures and touched off an inflationary spiral of unknown dimensions.[21] The easing of price supports, it might be noted, ignited nationwide riots in 1977 and poses a clear threat to do so again in the future.

Increases in population have been more than matched by rural migration to Cairo and Egypt's other commercial and industrial centers. The population of Cairo, approximately 3 million in 1960, is currently approaching the 14 million mark.[22] Housing shortages in Cairo have long passed the critical level and the city's utility infrastructure has expanded little since the early 1950s. A recent issue of *Al Mussawar,* for example, observed that one-third of Cairo's water network requires renovation and, in all probability, replacement.[23] Forty percent of the water pumped during peak periods, according to the article, is lost due to breakage in the mains and seepage problems. The article goes on to elaborate problems relating to Cairo's other utilities and suggests that the sewer system is in far worse condition than the water system. The problems of Cairo, it is important to stress, are the problems of Egypt. Cairo is the industrial, commercial, communications, and administrative hub of the nation. Everything goes through Cairo. Delays caused by congestion in the Cairo metroplex extract incalculable costs throughout the country and in all spheres of economic and social activity.

Population growth also means a growth in the labor force. The Egyptian labor force of 11.6 million in 1972 is expected to more than double by the turn of the century and to quadruple by the year 2225.[24] Beset with problems of underemployment at the present time, not to mention a shrinking market for export labor in the face of declining oil prices, Egypt's hopes for meeting the employment needs of future generations are totally contingent upon the development of a vigorous and expanding national economy.

The prospects for sustained economic development, unfortunately, are not bright. As things currently stand, Egypt is a debtor nation that maintains a precarious grip upon economic viability by relying upon revenues derived from tourism, the Suez Canal, foreign aid, oil, cotton, and the export of Egyptian labor to the oil-producing states of the Arab world. Virtually all of Egypt's major sources of hard currency are external to the industrial sector of the economy. They are also unstable. Revenues from tourism, for example, have largely been offset by the expenditures of Egyptians traveling abroad. Revenues derived from the export of petroleum are threatened by the declining price of oil on the world market and the sharp increases in Egypt's domestic consumption, consumption abetted by price supports for gasoline. If the rapid increase in domestic production is not offset by either constraints on consumption or increased production, or both, Egypt may again find itself a net importer of petroleum products.

Cotton revenues, to continue an all too bleak picture, are threatened by the flood of synthetic fibers on the world market and by the increased production of cotton in the Sudan and elsewhere. Remittances from the oil states have shrunk as a result of the drop in oil prices and are expected to decline even more over the next decade. And, to add a final note of pessimism to the economic picture, one finds little evidence that the massive infusions of American foreign aid into the Egyptian economy that have occurred since 1975 have done much either to correct its fundamental ills or to increase its productive capacity. Quite the contrary, much of the U.S. aid effort in Egypt is devoted to patching up what some AID officials believe to be a sinking ship. The role of U.S. aid is a critical factor in keeping the Egyptian economy afloat, yet, as things now stand, there is little evidence that the Egyptian economy will be any better able to stand on its own feet once the aid program stops.

President Mubarak suffers no illusions concerning the problems facing his nation. Indeed, his November 1985 address to the People's Assembly was a catalogue of Egypt's ills and an urgent plea for Egyptians to come together in finding solutions to those problems. Among other things, President Mubarak noted:

> We had before us (upon assuming office) the prospect of crumbling public services and utilities. The situation was the result of years of accumulated paralysis and neglect. Citizens complained of the situation from the moment they opened their eyes in the morning until they returned from work. The flow of water was inadequate and irregular. Electric current fluctuated, and extended blackouts were common. Communications moved at a snail's pace. Roads were impassable. Television was limited. The decay of the sewer system turned some streets and quarters into swamps. . . .
>
> Medical equipment in public hospitals is old and in short supply. Public services (bureaucracy) oppress the citizens with routine and delay. Free education has lost much of its effectiveness and the expense of college education is oppressive to Egyptian families. Then there are the problems of housing shortages, rising prices, vanishing goods, and of houses collapsing on their inhabitants. The list of problems our people complain of is endless, yet they are forced to put up with them.[25]

President Mubarak went on to note the widening gap between wages and prices, the decline in revenues from all of Egypt's sources of hard currency, the low productivity of Egyptian workers, the lethargy of the bureaucracy, and the trade imbalance during the past year when Egypt imported approximately $9 billion in goods and services while exporting only $4.5 billion in goods and materials including oil.

Egypt, then, has no choice but to make substantial progress in the areas of economic and social development if it is to meet even the most basic needs of a population projected to double within twenty years. Moreover, the cost of this development must be born by the present generation of Egyptians, a generation already severely taxed by the problems surveyed above. Just how much more of an economic burden can be imposed upon the present generation is a matter of some debate.

In facing the dual challenges of development and survival, Egypt must ultimately choose between a strategy of muddling through with massive infusions of loans and foreign assistance and a strategy of self-sacrifice and self-reliance.

President Mubarak's November 1985 speech to the People's Assembly minced few words in outlining the policy of self-sacrifice and self-reliance to be pursued by his regime.[26] The task, he stressed, was formidable but not impossible. Egypt's development, the President said, was not a matter of greater material sacrifice. It was a matter of greater individual effort and the rational use of Egypt's substantial resources. With greater effort and the rational use of Egypt's existing resources, President Mubarak stated, it should be possible to double Egypt's output of goods and services without placing additional burdens on the Egyptian population. The doubling of production, he assured the Egyptian population, would be more than adequate to ease Egypt's pressing economic and social burdens. It would place Egypt firmly on the road to prosperity and development. Moreover, the President continued, the doubling of effort would not place undue strain upon the Egyptian worker and the Egyptian bureaucrat. Egyptians, he stated frankly, do not work as hard as they might. In particular, he criticized the high levels of worker absenteeism in government service, bureaucratic disdain for the public, and widespread worker apathy. In this regard, he noted "by systematic work and respect for appointments we do not merely mean that the individual will be found in his place of work, but that he will approach his work with sincerity and with a spirit of responsibility and conscience." President Mubarak went on to indicate that worker apathy and lack of responsibility resulted in inordinately high levels of waste. Nine percent of Egypt's agricultural production, he noted, is lost to waste, a figure that jumps to 11 percent among perishable goods. A country that is dependent upon food imports, he stressed, can ill afford such waste.

Turning to a more rational use of Egypt's human and material resources, President Mubarak called for simplification of the morass of bureaucratic rules and regulations. Topping his list of needed changes were incentive programs that failed to distinguish between productive and nonproductive individuals and the bureaucratic red tape that has hamstrung efforts by the private sector to play a more vital role in the development of the Egyptian economy. He also outlined proposed changes in the public sector companies, acknowledging that "the public sector bears many burdens of the past, including fixed prices unrelated to rising costs of production, absorbing surplus labor from among the graduates, submitting to ministerial laws and decisions which restrict administrative discretion and limit the administrator's ability to use available talents and capacities by precluding them from discriminating between lazy and productive workers."[27]

To say that Egypt must solve its own problems and spearhead its own economic and social development is, given the intense bureaucratization of the Egyptian state, to say that the bureaucracy must spearhead Egypt's economic and social development. The revitalization of the private sector, while generating considerable activity in the areas of tourism, construction, banking, and real estate, has thus far been marginal to the long-range goals of Egyptian development.

Foreign assistance cannot replace the role of the bureaucracy in the developmental process either. Indeed, much of the potential benefit of the massive U.S. aid program in Egypt has been blunted by the poor interface between the respective bureaucratic establishments and their difficulty in agreeing upon common projects, priorities, and procedures. If foreign aid is to be effective, it must be presented in a manner that is compatible with Egyptian procedures and priorities.

If the Egyptian bureaucracy cannot or will not play a dynamic role in the economic and social development of Egypt, that development will be slow and halting, at best. It most assuredly will not be able to meet the needs of Egypt's growing population.

Unfortunately, many of the scholars and practitioners interviewed by the Al Ahram research team felt that the Egyptian bureaucracy, as presently formed, lacked the capacity to play a vital role in the developmental process. Many interviewees also questioned the willingness of the bureaucracy to play a decisive role in the developmental process. In their view, questions of motivation and morale had to be essential ingredients of any future reform effort.

Bureaucracies, understandably, are not self-reforming. The impetus and the sustained pressure for reform must come from President Mubarak. In his first six years in office, President Mubarak has taken the first step in this direction by publicizing the major problems confronting Egypt and the Egyptian bureaucracy. As he embarks upon his second term of office he must now act to solve those problems. If President Mubarak's call for bureaucratic reform degenerates into little more than a slogan, his domestic programs will falter, just as the domestic programs of Nasser and Sadat faltered before him.

Deep questions arise, however, concerning the willingness of the Mubarak government to initiate a thorough reform of the Egyptian bureaucracy. Four policy issues, in particular, cloud a timely and thorough reform of the bureaucracy.

The first issue concerns Egypt's growing level of unemployment and particularly intellectual unemployment, problems exacerbated by the ever-increasing flow of university graduates as well as by the return of expatriate workers from the oil states. While calling for bureaucratic efficiency and recognizing that the bureaucracy is severely overstaffed, President Mubarak has found it necessary, at least temporarily, to continue the long-established practice of using the bureaucracy as a safety valve to ease the pressures of excessive unemployment. Using the bureaucracy as a welfare system is clearly antithetical to bureaucratic efficiency.

A second issue likely to delay bureaucratic reform during President Mubarak's second term in office is the intense pressure that he has received from the United States and the International Monetary Fund to eliminate price supports and to rationalize Egypt's currency policy, policies that many observers fear will result in a surge of inflation. A substantial reduction in price supports could also trigger waves of political unrest reminiscent of the 1977 riots sparked by Sadat's efforts to reduce price supports. As current bureaucratic salaries hover around the subsistence level, a reduction in price supports would destroy the tenuous economic position of the majority of Egypt's salaried workforce unless it were matched by a corresponding increase in government salaries. Providing large salary increases to the bureaucracy as presently constituted, however, would be tremendously expensive and, in many ways, would absorb the savings occasioned by the reduction in price supports. Indeed, unless increases in bureaucratic salaries were part of a thorough and far-reaching reform program, the increase in bureaucratic salaries would represent little more than a new though less visible subsidy. Reinforcing this view is the fact that bureaucratic reform, and particularly the reduction of the size of the bureaucracy, is part and parcel of the economic reform package being urged upon Egypt and other states of the Third World by the International Monetary Fund.[28] Thus far President Mubarak has vowed to resist radical economic reforms that would cause undue hardship to the Egyptian population. While President Mubarak's posture on economic reform does not preclude independent reform of the bureaucracy, the two issues are so intertwined that one may be difficult without the other.

Third, the Mubarak regime may find it difficult to pursue far-reaching bureaucratic reform before resolving the debate between the public and private sectors of the Egyptian economy. Indeed, the logical first step in bureaucratic reform would be deciding precisely what role the bureaucracy is to play during the coming decade. One would anticipate, for example, that an expansion of the private sector would result in a corresponding reduction of the public sector, thereby easing the burden of bureaucratic reform. On the negative side, however, one might also anticipate that the privatization of public sector companies would result in a drastic paring of employees, thereby raising the spector of increased unemployment and the resultant increase of political tensions. Be this as it may, the debate concerning the proper balance between the public and private sectors of the Egyptian economy is far from being resolved. Just how far it is from being resolved is indicated by the following excerpt from a Mubarak interview conducted by *Al Watan Al Arabi* in November of 1987.

I wonder about those who advocate selling the public sector, because this would be a dangerous step taken at the cost of the simple citizen, because the private sector operates according to the needs of the market, and its prices are high. So what is the simple citizen to do? Frankly, he will starve. From here starts social envy and crime flourishes. This envy has serious effects on the social structure. The public sector regulates the private one, thus offering goods to the public at reasonable prices, because state control is a must. Selling the public sector would create a socio-economic problem. I am careful to maintain social peace and balance. These are the fundamentals for me. So I reiterate that the public sector is an essential foundation of the Egyptian social and economic structure. As for tourism, we have opened the door for investments and handed over several hotels to the private sector. But as for national industries essential for further production, they must remain in public ownership.[29]

Finally, progress toward bureaucratic reform may be slowed by President Mubarak's most laudable efforts at democratic reform. Political views are expressed more freely in Egypt today than at any time since the revolution. Political parties compete for representation in the National Assembly and, in so doing, follow the classic democratic practice of advocating policies likely to garner a majority of the votes. In this regard, it must be noted that the Egyptian bureaucracy is a large and critical constituency. The bureaucracy is valued by many of its members as a security system. Any effort to radically transform the security/welfare provisions of the bureaucracy could well be politically damaging to the dominant position of President Mubarak's National Democratic Party.

The policy considerations that constrain President Mubarak's desire for far-reaching bureaucratic reform are very real and are not easily resolved. The cruel fact remains, however, that bureaucratic reform is central to a resolution of the economic and social crises that currently rend Egyptian society.

2

❧

The Bureaucratic Milieu

Outlining the challenges that confront Egypt and the Egyptian bureaucracy in their quest for economic and social development is a relatively easy task. It is a far more difficult task to assess the capacity of the Egyptian bureaucracy to meet those challenges. What attributes must the Egyptian bureaucracy possess if it is to meet the challenges of the coming decade?

Theoretical and empirical works concerning the assessment of bureaucratic capacity remain in their infancy.[1] Nevertheless, broad agreement exists that bureaucratic capacity is a function of at least four key variables: structural or organizational variables, behavioral variables, client-interaction variables, and environmental variables. The Al Ahram project focused on the behavioral dimensions of bureaucratic capacity: the behavior of administrators and the attitudes, opinions, and values that shape that behavior. Behavior, however, does not occur in a vacuum. As later analysis will reveal, the behavior of Egyptian officials is profoundly influenced by their organizational setting as well as by various dimensions of their larger political, economic, and social environment. The present chapter will set the stage for the ensuing analysis of Egyptian bureaucratic behavior (chapters 3 through 7) by outlining the major institutional and environmental constraints under which the bureaucracy must labor.

Structural Constraints on Developmental Capacity

Bureaucratic structure covers a multitude of sins relating to the mechanics and organization of the bureaucracy and its respective

19

units. Included within the structural category one finds classic administrative concerns such as the allocation of functions and responsibilities, authority hierarchies, staffing, formal communications, coordination between and within units, recruitment, training, salaries, incentives, and promotions. Also falling within the structural category are matters of equipment, the physical work environment, and related items of an inanimate nature which impact on the administrative process.

Structural concerns influence the developmental capacity of a bureaucracy in at least two ways. First, the structural arrangement of a bureaucracy influences its physical capacity to execute tasks. The more rational the administrative structure of a bureaucracy, the greater its potential capacity to execute complex tasks efficiently. Second, the structural arrangements of the bureaucracy often play a role in shaping the behavior of administrators. The later point will be a recurring theme throughout the analytical chapters.

An analysis of the structural problems limiting the ability of the Egyptian bureaucracy to operate efficiently logically begins with an examination of the organizational integrity of the bureaucracy as a total entity. Just how "rational" is the organizational structure of the Egyptian bureaucracy?

The answer to this question, as one might anticipate, does not generate confidence in the ability of the Egyptian bureaucracy to play a dynamic role in the developmental process. The bureaucratic establishment in Egypt consists of three distinct groups of officialdom: the mainline ministries, the public agencies and public corporations, and the provincial and local governments. The mainline ministries were inherited from the monarchy more or less intact and, aside from growing in number, have changed little in their organizational structure over the past three decades.

With the advent of the socialization laws of 1961, Egypt's major commercial and manufacturing enterprises were nationalized and became part and parcel of the bureaucratic establishment. Although the newly incorporated public corporations were technically distinct from the mainline bureaucracies, the desire of the Nasser regime to centralize its control over its disparate bureaucratic apparatus enabled the relevant ministers to exert considerable authority over the public organizations under their jurisdiction.[2] Shortly after the advent of the Sadat regime, however, administrative decentralization became the order of the day. This process is succinctly described by Richard Nyrop.

Under the old system there were sixty-two public authorities and public service organizations in charge of about 600 public companies. The public service organizations provided basic services, e.g., transportation, health care, and communications at pre-set, reduced fees and with no profits. The public authorities were constituted as holding companies to oversee subsidiary enterprises grouped together by similarity of function. Basically the public authorities were entrusted with the functions of planning, budgeting, advising, and coordinating for the companies placed under enterprises with a profit motive. The sixty-two authorities and organizations were placed under functionally appropriate ministries that were charged with planning, budgeting, and coordinating and with monthly "follow up" activities to supervise implementation. In 1975, however, Law Number 1167 abolished the public authorities in favor of supreme sectoral councils, thus severing the control linkages between the ministries and the public companies. These companies were left to operate freely without institutional supervision. Similarly the relationships between the ministries and the public service organizations were relaxed, ostensibly to promote flexibility and efficiency. These policies of decentralization have had mixed results. Operating in an organizational vacuum, there has been a decline in accountability and control, without a perceptible increase in productivity and quality. In certain cases the regime's policy of decentralization has provided opportunities for private enrichment and corruption.[3]

The third layer of bureaucracy consists of the twenty-six provincial administrators as well as *markaz* (center) and *garyah* (village) administrators who are appointed by the provincial governors. As in the case of the public agencies and public companies, the Sadat era witnessed a decentralization of control over the provincial bureaucracies. Indeed, in 1982 the Ministry of Local Government was abolished, creating a situation in which direct ministerial control over the provincial bureaucracies was weakened to the breaking point.[4]

The organizational structure of the Egyptian bureaucracy, then, is most unwieldy. It is not entirely clear that the right hand knows what the left hand is doing. Functions between agencies overlap and coordination between bureaucratic units is problematic, at best. Organizational problems, however, are merely the tip of the structural iceberg. Few structural problems are as debilitating to the overall performance of the Egyptian bureaucracy as the problem of red tape, a concept referred to in Egypt as "routine." Little in Egypt is achieved without a multitude of clearances, signatures, permits, and stamps. Laws and regulations are complex, vague, and often contradictory. Authority is heavily centralized in the hands of senior officials, causing delays and bottlenecks as issues easily resolved by subordinates await consideration by the supervisor. The routine and red tape of the Egyptian bureaucracy often render even the most simple acts complex. In his 1985 speech to the People's Assembly, President Mubarak repeatedly cited bureaucratic rigidity and red tape as major factors discouraging economic growth in Egypt.[5] Bureaucratic routine, he said, had slowed development of the private sector, discouraged Egyptian expatriates from depositing their savings in Egyptian banks, and obstructed cooperation between the government and the public.

According to Nazih Ayubi and Samir Youssef, two of the Egyptian bureaucracy's most severe critics, the Egyptian bureaucracy suffers from a multitude of other structural defects as well.[6] Offices are overstaffed and the match between skill and functions is said to be random at best. Coordination between units is poor. Functions overlap, resulting in both conflict between units and a tendency for important tasks to get lost in the shuffle. The quality of information available to officials is not always high either. Ramzi Zaki, for example, reports that the bureaucracy lacks clear information on the distribution of income in Egypt, a statistic of critical importance to Egypt's developmental efforts.[7] The Al Ahram project itself was unable to get a clear picture of how public corporations are evaluated in terms of their relative effectiveness.

The Egyptian bureaucracy is also condemned for the low skill level of its workers, a circumstance aggravated by low salary levels and recruitment policies designed to provide employment for the graduates of Egypt's many universities. Evaluation procedures are rigid and fail to distinguish between productive and nonproductive workers.[8] The firing of nonproductive workers is theoretically possible, yet is such an arduous process that few administrators find it worth their effort.[9]

Finally, the developmental capacity of the Egyptian bureaucracy is hampered by its physical structure. Offices tend to be scattered, aggravating an already difficult communications process. Data processing equipment remains rudimentary and inadequate in most areas. Working conditions tend to be poor and overcrowded.

Structural problems in the Egyptian bureaucracy, needless to say, do influence the behavior of Egyptian officials and workers. Low salary levels depress worker morale and force most government employees to seek second or even third jobs. Hierarchical authority patterns reinforce the concentration of authority by supervisory of-ficials and discourage the assumption of responsibility by their subor-dinates. Crowded work conditions and overstaffing contribute to complaints of worker apathy and indifference. This is not to suggest that the behavioral problems confronting the Egyptian bureaucracy are solely the result of structural inadequacies. This is far from the case, but structural problems are a contributing factor.

The Environment of Bureaucracy in Egypt: Economics

The bureaucratic environment in Egypt consists of three basic components: the economic environment, the political environment, and the public environment. The economic environment in which the Egyptian bureaucracy operates requires little elaboration. Egypt is a poor country with few natural resources that currently imports twice as much as it exports. Administrative expenses already consume a lion's share of the state budget. No elasticity remains in the budget to increase salaries or to initiate expensive incentive programs. To the contrary, virtually all analyses of Egypt's financial situation call for a sharp reduction in government expenditures. Any efforts to increase productivity via monetary incentives would almost certainly have to be implemented within existing budget allocations. This may be a difficult task, for as later analysis will indicate, salaries are the number one source of job dissatisfaction within the bureaucracy.

A second economic fact of life confronting the Egyptian bu-reaucracy is that salaries in the private sector and in the oil states are often many times higher than corresponding salaries in government service. The bureaucracy, accordingly, suffers a perpetual drain of talent and experience to the private sector and to the Gulf. Such defections clearly reduce the capacity of the bureaucracy to play a dynamic role in the developmental process.

Yet a third element in the economic environment is the steady rise in inflation that has beset Egypt during the past decade. While government expenditures more than quadrupled between 1973 and 1980, the purchasing power of salaried employees steadily declined in spite of increases in salary levels designed to cope with inflationary pressures.[10] Thus at the same time that President Mubarak complains that salaries are approaching levels in "some developed states" and pose a threat to the financial viability of the government, some 89 percent of the officials surveyed in the Al Ahram study found it necessary to maintain a second job. Reflecting the cruel complexities of Egyptian economics, President Mubarak's assessment of the high cost of Egyptian labor in the government sector was based upon total costs including salaries, family allowances, incentives, insurance schemes, and various support programs. Employee assessments of their purchasing power—and their sense of relative deprivation vis-à-vis the private sector—is based on take-home pay.

To this complex and unhappy picture, one must add the problem of government price supports which jumped from some £E 9,000,000 in 1961, to £E 40,000,000 in 1971, to £E 2,000,000,000 in 1982. Originally instituted to alleviate the hardships and dislocations of World War II, the system of price supports for basic foods increased gradually during the 1960s, constituting an important element of Egypt's socialist economic and welfare policies. The era of *infitah,* however, triggered an era of spiraling inflation abetted by the decline of the Egyptian pound from 40 piasters to a dollar to 80 piasters to a dollar within a period of a few months and an equally dramatic rise in the cost of Egyptian imports resulting from the escalation of oil prices and worldwide inflation.[11] Increases in price supports for basic commodities thus became an essential element in preserving the viability of government salaries, not to mention the survival of Egypt's poor.

In the view of USAID officials and the International Monetary Fund, the reduction if not total elimination of price supports is an inescapable economic necessity. Any alteration in price supports, however, could seriously disrupt the morale of the bureaucracy, such as it is, and lead to even greater defections to the private sector. If the Egyptian bureaucracy is to play an effective role in the developmental process, it can ill afford a further deterioration of its morale or increased defections of its experienced cadres.

The Environment of Egyptian Bureaucracy: Politics

In examining the influence of politics on the Egyptian bureaucracy, the first point to be noted is that the bureaucracy executes decisions made by the political elite. If the decisions of Egypt's leaders lack clarity or if priorities are vague and shifting, the bureaucracy may well flounder in a sea of uncertainty. While some units will be paralyzed by lack of direction, others will jump from priority to priority in a perpetual guessing game while still others pursue the pet projects of their leaders in an idiosyncratic and uncoordinated manner. The Egyptian political system, in all candor, has not provided the bureaucracy with either clear directions or clear priorities, a phenomenon manifest in the morass of government rules and procedures, not to mention government ambivalence on such crucial issues as the graduates policy and the interaction between the public and private sectors.

In much the same manner, Egypt's political leaders have yet to clarify their priorities concerning the function of the bureaucracy. Specifically, the government must choose between a bureaucracy capable of playing a reasonably efficient and dynamic role in the developmental process and a bureaucracy designed to augment social welfare by absorbing successive generations of graduates. They cannot have it both ways. The social welfare orientation of previous Egyptian governments has resulted in the severe overstaffing of the bureaucracy and has precluded agencies from implementing evaluation procedures that distinguish between productivity and slough. Moreover, government salaries reflect a desire to provide a survival wage to the many rather than a competitive wage to a leaner yet more efficient bureaucratic cadre. Such policies bode ill for the developmental capacity of the Egyptian bureaucracy.

Also, Egypt's political leaders have contributed to the problems of the Egyptian bureaucracy by demanding more than the bureaucracy could reasonably deliver. They have also failed to provide the resources necessary to meet those demands. Demands that exceed resources are futile. In this regard it need only be noted that the demands placed upon the bureaucracy during the Nasser regime so overwhelmed the frail structure of the bureaucracy that it continues to suffer from organizational confusion and from behavior patterns tailored to survival rather than productivity. Such behavior patterns are the subject of considerable attention in later stages of the analysis.

Moreover, Egyptian politicians have not been reluctant to bend the rules of the bureaucracy to benefit friends and supporters. Politicians do secure positions for clients and do influence the evaluation (and disciplining) thereof. Some 10 percent of the respondents in the

Al Ahram project, for example, willingly indicated that they received their positions via *wasta*. Such *wasta* or influence may have been internal to the bureaucracy rather than political in nature, but it does indicate that the process is alive and well. Politics has also entered the Egyptian bureaucracy in ideological guise. The Nasser regime demanded, but did not receive, a bureaucracy imbued with a socialist ideology. Key bureaucratic positions were placed in the hands of individuals judged loyal to the regime, a policy repeated by President Sadat. This is not to suggest that Egyptian leaders are unique in making political and ideological loyalty a prime ingredient in bureaucratic appointments, but merely that such policies do have a debilitating influence on bureaucratic performance.

Finally, Egyptian politicans have hamstrung the Egyptian bureaucracy via their efforts to dominate and control the bureaucracy. With the advent of state socialism in the beginning of the 1960s, the Egyptian government manifested a marked tendency for overplanning and overcontrol. In part, such overplanning resulted from a desire to maximize the developmental potential of existing resources in the briefest time possible. It also reflected the socialist orientation of the regime as well as a tendency of Egyptian politicians and planners to compensate for the perceived inadequacies of the bureaucracy by forcing bureaucratic units to work within the confines of rigid plans and controls. The plans and controls, however, were too inflexible and too complex. They stifled the bureaucracy by limiting its scope for decentralized decision making and by demanding levels of coordination and timing that the bureaucracy could not achieve. Frustrated by excessive demands and controls, the bureaucracy retreated behind a wall of regulation and routine. In regard to the debilitating impact of excessive controls on public sector companies, Samir Youssef writes: "This type of control encourages rigidity in applying rules and regulations in order to avoid questioning later on by the agency's staff, even if it results in losses. This approach, an extension of the work system in government bureaucracies, can be fatal and self-defeating in productive enterprises. If public sector companies were granted enough autonomy and freed from the cumbersome system of rules and regulations, their control could be based on results achieved. . . ."[12] Centralized planning in the sense of five-year plans was disrupted by the June war of 1967 and further disrupted by the *infitah* policies of the 1970s, policies which resulted in a unique blend of centralized planning in the public sector and laissez-faire policies in the private sector. In effect, this mix of planning and laissez-faire policies may have provided Egypt with the worst of both worlds.[13]

President Mubarak is well aware of the debilitating influence of political pressures on bureaucratic peformance and has recently issued directives to ease political interference in the public sector companies. Among other things, President Mubarak has enjoined the ministries from issuing any new decisions restricting the administrative autonomy of public sector projects. He has similarly instructed the ministries to give the administrators of public sector companies the ability to rationalize their human talent via a merit-oriented use of incentives and punishments. These are small steps with which to address a major problem, but they do represent acknowledgement of the problem, and they are steps in the right direction.

The Bureaucratic Environment in Egypt: The Masses

The public is the target of bureaucratic activity. In Third World states such as Egypt, the public is also the primary focus of economic and social modernization. It is the bureaucracy that must sell development to the masses and encourage mass involvement in the economic and social goals of the state. As part and parcel of this process, the bureaucracy must take the lead in building mass confidence in the government. It must persuade the masses that the government can solve the economic and social problems confronting the state and its citizens. The ability of a bureaucracy to play a dynamic role in the developmental process, then, is inextricably linked to levels of trust and confidence between the bureaucracy and its clients. A bureaucracy that encounters public doubt and resistance at every turn will find its task difficult, indeed. Because of the centrality of mass/bureaucratic relations to economic development in Egypt, the topic will be approached from two perspectives. The current discussion of the mass environment will focus on the historical patterns of interaction between the bureaucracy and the masses. Chapter 6, in turn, will examine bureaucratic attitudes toward the public.

The modern history of bureaucracy in Egypt begins with the reign of Mohammed Ali and his attempts to transform Egypt into a military base for his imperial aspirations. Most government officials during this period were of Turkish or Mamluke origin. Being of foreign origin, they identified with and adopted the values of Mohammed Ali's court. Collectively, the political elite and the bureaucracy formed a single unit dedicated to the rule of the masses. As Lane described the period in his *Manners and Customs of the Modern Egyptians,* services were few and taxes were many.[14] Government officials were arbitrary, capricious, and oppressive. Mass distrust of the bureaucracy was a rational response to the realities of the period; deception was a matter of survival.

With the advent of the British period, native Egyptians were encouraged to enter government service as the British sought to provide Mohammed Ali's less-ambitious but equally resplendent heirs with the foundations of a modern state. Educational institutions were established to prepare the foundations of a bureaucratic career. Indeed, it was during this period that the link between the university and government service was first established in Egypt, a link that would find its culmination in Nasser's graduates policy. Most Egyptians to enter the bureaucracy during this period were the sons of aristocrats and land owners who were anxious to place their progeny on the path to power and economic security. The rush to the bureaucracy was also augmented by the growing scarcity of land and the absence of a viable manufacturing sector. Many sons of the upper classes had little choice other than a bureaucratic career. Upon completion of their studies they turned to the bureaucracy as naturally as day turns to night. The gap between the bureaucracy and the masses, however, remained large. One aristocracy had merely been replaced by another.

The revolution of 1952 was to radically alter the social composition of the bureaucracy. Free education, in conjunction with the graduates policy, transformed the bureaucracy into a mass-based institution, albeit an institution staffed by a highly educated segment of Egyptian society. A bureaucratic career, nevertheless, continued to be the premier avenue of economic and political security for educated Egyptians. Indeed, under the era of socialism, the employment alternatives for educated Egyptians were even more limited than they had been under the monarchy. Bureaucratic positions also retained their traditional prestige in the eye of the public, a circumstance reflected in the popular saying "better to be a bureaucrat than grovel in their dust."

Relations between the bureaucracy and the masses during the Nasser era were strained by a growing casualness or indifference on the part of many officials. This casualness was influenced by both the graduates policy which made bureaucratic appointments a "right" of college graduates as well as by parallel socialist legislation that made it exceptionally difficult for supervisors to remove officials from their positions once appointed. The growth of such attitudes, in combination with the structural dislocations occasioned by the rush to socialism, resulted in a tangible decline in the level of bureaucratic services. The decline in services, moreover, was made all the more perceptible by Nasser's welfare rhetoric. Nasser's promises of a socialist nirvana stimulated an increase in mass expectations that simply could not be fulfilled by the bureaucracy. The masses were thus demanding more but receiving less.

As the quality of bureaucratic performance declined during the socialist era, the long-established alliance between the bureaucracy and the political elite gave way to a tacit alliance between the political elite and the masses. Both began to view the bureaucracy as the main obstacle to the attainment of Nasser's socialist dream.

Relations between the masses and bureaucracy were to improve little during the Sadat era. The alliance between the masses and the political elite remained intact, with Sadat himself leading the charge against the bureaucracy. Many of the bureaucracy's more experienced members migrated to the public sector or to the oil states, further reducing the level of public service. Bureaucratic concerns toward public service, such as they were, also suffered from the growing disparity between salaries in the public sector and salaries in the private sector. Low morale and public service seldom go hand in hand.

The mass environment confronting the Egyptian bureaucracy as it enters the second term of the Mubarak era, then, is an environment marked by considerable skepticism. The tacit alliance between the political elite and the masses that emerged during the Nasser regime remains very much intact. It is the bureaucracy that has been the scapegoat for the social and economic crises of the past four decades. Using the bureaucracy as a whipping boy for Egypt's social and economic ills, unfortunately, has not been without its costs. To the contrary, President Mubarak must now go before the Egyptian public and urge them to have faith in their bureaucracy and in its ability to solve their massive economic and social problems. In effect, he is calling upon the masses to set aside generations of skepticism and to embrace the bureaucracy as the instrument of national salvation. They may be hesitant to do so.

Before moving to the next topic, it must be stressed that interaction between the bureaucracy and the masses is a two-way process. Mass demands upon the bureaucracy have grown steadily in the four decades of the Egyptian revolution. Moreover, there is little if any evidence that mass demands have been matched by increases in public cooperation and support. To the contrary, the socialist culture of the 1950s and 1960s spawned an attitude of public dependency upon government services. What Egypt's citizens previously did for themselves or did without, they now demanded from the government. In a similar manner, if the Egyptian bureaucracy is open to charges of favoritism and corruption, one explanation of this culpability lies in the pervasive drive of the masses to circumvent existing rules by pressing friends and relatives in the bureaucracy to do their bidding.[15]

Some Behavioral Requisites of Developmental Bureaucracies

The literatures of public administration, developmental administration, and political development have achieved a high level of consensus concerning four behavioral attributes that a bureaucracy should possess if it is to become a reasonably effective instrument of development: drive, innovation, flexibility, and rapport with the masses.[16] The listing of such requisites does not suggest that their presence provides a sufficient condition for development. A mere listing of variables does not suggest how much of a given quantity is necessary for development or how the diverse requisite variables do or should interact in the development process either. At best, the listing of variables thought to be important to the developmental process is but the first step in theory building, and a small step at that. It is, however, a beginning, and it does provide a basis for examining the problems of the Egyptian bureaucracy in a framework that builds upon the experience of other states and that contributes to the general literatures of political development and comparative administration.

Drive

The list of bureaucratic attributes requisite for economic and social development is headed by the need for sufficient drive or energy to execute assigned tasks in a timely and efficient manner. A sluggish bureaucracy that finds it difficult to keep pace with the ongoing activities required to maintain the status quo can hardly be expected to play a dynamic role in the areas of economic and social development. The capacity of a bureaucracy to play a dynamic role in the developmental process would clearly be enhanced by a sizable cadre of individuals imbued with a deep sense of achievement motivation or work ethic. One would also hope that achievement values would permeate the work culture or group dynamic of the bureaucracy. Quite clearly, a bureaucracy staffed by high achievers working in a professionally oriented group environment stands a far better chance of playing a vigorous role in the developmental process than a bureaucracy staffed by officials who find their duties an imposition on their time and who use their working hours to read the papers, chat with friends, and run family errands. At the very least, the need for drive or energy requires a bureaucracy that is professional in the performance of its tasks. Apathy is the foe of development. If drive and energy are not present within the bureaucracy, motivational techniques must be developed and refined to provide the drive and energy required by the developmental process.

Innovation

Just as development is linked to drive and energy, it is also linked to the need for innovation and risk taking. Simply stated, the greater the role a bureaucracy must play in the economic and social development of a society, the more crucial it becomes that the members of that bureaucracy have a capacity to find new and innovative approaches to the social and economic problems besetting that society. Equally important, members of the bureaucracy must be willing to take the risks necessary to see their ideas become policy. It should be stressed that innovation is not merely the province of the planners at the pinnacle of the bureaucratic hierarchy. Innovation must permeate the entire bureaucratic apparatus. Lower levels of the bureaucracy are on the firing line of policy execution, the point at which the opportunities for innovation may be the most visible and the easiest to implement. Similarly, supervisors must be willing to implement innovations suggested by their subordinates and to pass new ideas up the administrative hierarchy.

Flexibility

Flexibility represents a third bureaucratic requisite for development. Flexible bureaucracies are better able to coordinate the execution of projects than their less-flexible counterparts. They also use available talent more effectively than rigid bureaucracies, and they generally improve the climate of public relations by sparing clients interminable periods of waiting required to plead their case, regardless of how small, before remote officials with crowded agendas and limited hours. Bureaucratic flexibility also enhances the flow of ideas within the bureaucracy, thereby facilitating both innovation and the transfer of technology.

Flexible bureaucracies, from a behavioral perspective, are marked by the willingness of supervisors to delegate authority to their subordinates and the willingness of subordinates to accept the responsibility thus delegated. They are also marked by minimal red tape and by the uninhibited flow of communications between and within bureaucratic units.

Rapport with the Public

In outlining the developmental requisites of a bureaucracy it is difficult to overemphasize the need for cooperation between the bureaucracy and the public it was ostensibly designed to serve. As noted in earlier discussion, is it often incumbent upon the bureaucracy to sell development to its clients, many of whom may fear or be antagonistic to change. Moreover, for its programs to be effective, the bureaucracy must enlist the cooperation of the public. Bureaucratic efforts to implement programs among a hostile population will be slow to reach fruition, at best. It should also be noted that the need for rapport with the public blurs the line between the maintenance and the developmental roles of the bureaucracy, for bureaucratic resources and energies are finite. The lack of mass cooperation in the execution of the maintenance functions of the bureaucracy absorbs energies and resources that might otherwise be available for development.

Other Important Variables

In addition to the four behavioral variables discussed above, the developmental capacity of a bureaucracy appears to be influenced by other behavioral variables as well. Questions of job satisfaction and favoritism, for example, play a prominent role in most analyses of bureaucratic behavior in Egypt. The relevant theoretical literature, however, lacks consensus on these issues, and it is difficult to place them in the category of prerequisites. In the view of many scholars, low job satisfaction reduces bureaucratic performance by reinforcing apathy among officials, by contributing to low group morale, by reducing concern for client satisfaction, and by creating a high rate of turnover within the bureaucracy. For others such as Frederick Herzberg, the crucial variable is not job dissatisfaction, but job satisfaction. While not disputing that poor morale can depress performance, Herzberg argues that merely removing the negative attributes of a job may not be sufficient to increase productivity. Motivation, he argues, is better studied via indicators of job satisfaction.[17] Chapter 5 examines this hypothesis in some detail.

In much the same manner, one could intuitively argue that favoritism and its variants such as interventionism (*wasta*) and nepotism are said to disrupt bureaucratic performance by blunting the logic of merit-based recruitment and evaluation processes as well as by undermining public confidence in the objectivity and impartiality of the bureaucracy. Problems of favoritism (and corruption) also reinforce bureaucratic rigidity by inducing the need for multiple clearances and other structural mechanisms designed to curb what is essentially a behavioral problem. A contrary position, however, suggests that favoritism and corruption ease the problems of bureaucratic rigidity. Favoritism, in this view, overcomes the worst effects of bureaucratic rigidity by shifting attention from formal to informal channels of communication.

Bureaucratic Behavior and Bureaucratic Culture in Egypt

President Mubarak's 1985 speech to the People's Assembly suggested that Egypt's bureaucracy suffers deficiencies in each of the six behavioral areas surveyed above. The main theme of his address, as noted earlier, was the need for greater productivity among Egyptians in general and within the government service in particular.[18] He criticized the rigidity of the bureaucracy and the reluctance of officials to shoulder responsibility. He decried the lack of public confidence in the bureaucracy and stressed the urgent need to increase cooperation between the bureaucracy and the public. In terms of the need for greater innovation and risk taking, President Mubarak announced that he had ordered that managers with a record of boldness and courage be assigned responsibility for the more sluggish of Egypt's public sector companies.

Few Egyptians would argue with the premise that their bureaucracy is sluggish, rigid, noninnovative, riddled with favoritism, and lacks concern for public service. Such observations are part and parcel of daily life in Egypt. Some Egyptian sociologists, however, suggest that the problem goes beyond the level of individual behavior and has become enmeshed in a bureaucratic culture that sets the norms of bureaucratic behavior; a culture into which new recruits are socialized and to which they are expected to conform.[19]

According to this view, Egyptian bureaucratic culture consists of at least seven basic components. Topping the list is the bureaucrat's unquestioning respect for authority. Supervisors adopt a superior attitude toward their subordinates, and subordinates respond with obsequiousness and flattery. Subordinates who cause trouble or lack the requisite servility may well find their career patterns limited. An eloquent portrayal of the relationship between superiors and subordinates appeared in a recent issue of the *Egyptian Gazette*.

> It is not indeed surprising that a government official should strive by all possible means to become a manager or a director-general of a department considering the manifold accompaniments of such a leading post. In the first place a manager is given a large office, nicely equipped with the most up-to-date furniture, a telephone neatly placed beside his enormous desk, a huge air conditioning apparatus. . . .
>
> But these material advantages are in fact nothing compared to the moral privileges accruing from such a splendid post. Not only are juniors over zealous to glorify the attributes of the infallible exalted man, but they are even more eager to vilify whoever had preceded him in the post.
>
> No sooner is an official promoted to the post of manager than

he ceases to accomplish any constructive work. His primary concern is to receive the compliments indiscriminately leveled at him from every quarter, and to smile with condescending magnanimity at the servile flattery lavished at him by his former colleagues.

Such a state of affairs has naturally developed out of a corrupt system of bureaucracy fostered and consolidated over the years, as a result of a deeply rooted fear in the hearts of juniors towards their superiors. Managers have actually capitalized on this fear in order to force more submission and humility on already humble juniors and to extort from them every possible kind of service and every conceivable kind of flattery.

With such managerial and moral accouterments adorning the post of manager, it is only natural that officials should be vying with one another to attain this post through all means available, not excluding hypocrisy, bribery, backbiting, double dealing and deception.[20]

Extreme deference to authority, it is important to stress, does not mean that job-related commands issued by the supervisor will be expedited. Quite to the contrary, a deference-oriented culture merely requires that subordinates show deference to authority figures. It does not require that they engage in hard labor. Egyptian culture, both popular and bureaucratic, is replete with terms of deference that convey the facade of submission while totally ignoring its spirit. It is not in vain that Egypt has survived centuries of foreign domination.

The second and third components of bureaucratic culture are norms limiting productivity and norms reinforcing an excessive concern for job security.[21] Both sets of norms are reflected in the bureaucratic proverb "the more you work, the more errors you make." The security of a bureaucratic position is more easily shattered by sins of commission than by sins of omission. Lack of effort is the norm and is to be expected. It is vague, nebulous, and difficult to punish. In reality, it causes few problems. Innovation and the aggressive pursuit of job goals, on the other hand, run the risk of error, of stepping on toes, of inadvertently upstaging the supervisor, of highlighting the lethargy of peers, and of generally disrupting the tranquillity of office routine. This is not to suggest that all Egyptian officials lack the foresight and drive required of a development-oriented bureaucracy. This clearly is not the case. Discussions of culture, however, center on the norm, not the exception.

Both the pervasive concern for job security and the existence of group norms against work figured prominently in earlier analyses of the Egyptian bureaucracy including Morroe Berger's *Bureaucracy and Society in Egypt* and Ayubi's *Bureaucracy and Politics in Contemporary Egypt*.[22] A sample of Ayubi's caustic appraisal of work norms in Egypt is provided in the following passage from his "Bureaucratic Inflation and Administrative Inefficiency."

> On average, the Egyptian civil servant was estimated to 'work' solidly only for a period of between twenty minutes and two hours every working day. Other amenities may also be provided: a shoe-shine man may pass by the offices to offer his services, and sometimes the odd vendor or two will also pass by, selling date-stuffed rolls or soap, perfume or mothballs, shoelaces or safety-pins. Then all of a sudden, a great rush will be seen and the offices will be almost entirely deserted: in an hour or so, cheerful faces will reappear as the officials return bearing their loot—oil, meat, chickens, olives, detergent, soap, and whatever else may happen to be available that day at the consumer cooperative of that particular government department.[23]

The fourth and fifth components of Egyptian bureaucratic culture focus on the rigid application of rules and the concomitant norm of resisting change in established routines. Following established procedures and routines is easy. It precludes argument and it avoids personal risk. The complexity of Egyptian procedures and routines is such that a ready and plausible excuse can be found for noncompliance with the demands of superiors and clients alike. Rule complexity provides a sword and a shield against both. Later analysis will provide some interesting data on this subject.

A sixth component of Egyptian bureaucratic culture is to be found in the condescension of bureaucrats toward the masses. Egyptian bureaucrats tend to view themselves as the granter of services rather than as the servants of the people. This attitude finds its roots in the historical position of the Egyptian bureaucracy as well as in the fact that the bureaucracy represents a highly educated strata within a poorly educated society. Whatever its cause, the superior attitude of the bureaucracy toward the masses does little to enhance rapport between the two entities. This topic finds elaboration in chapter 6.

The final component of Egyptian bureaucratic culture is the

corporate awareness of the bureaucracy. The norms of the bureaucracy stress protecting its members and concealing their mistakes. The bureaucracy also resists attacks on its prerogatives. In this regard, one might recall the earlier statement of the director of USAID in Egypt concerning the resistance of the Egyptian bureaucracy to both the Egyptian private sector and to the initiatives of the USAID program in Egypt.

The Origins of Bureaucratic Culture in Egypt

In sum, then, bureaucratic culture in Egypt appears to be antithetical to the norms and values that a bureaucracy must possess if it is to play a vital role in the developmental process. If existing norms and values are to be modified, it is essential that some consideration be given to their origins.

In part, the components of bureaucratic culture surveyed above find their origin in the venerated bureaucratic traditions of Egypt, traditions that return to the Pharaohs. The exalted position of bureaucrats, and their disdain for the masses have long been features of bureaucracy in Egypt. Historical and social traditions also contribute to the dominance of superiors and the deference of subordinates. Indeed, the superiority-subservience syndrome would seem to be built upon three historical and cultural traditions. First, the rulers of Egypt, whether indigenous or foreign, ruled the land as autocrats. Authority was the prerogative of Pharaohs, pashas, kings, and presidents. It flowed from the top down and brooked little tolerance for democratic decision making, political or otherwise. Second, the roots of Egyptian culture are patriarchal in nature. The Egyptian father is the lord and master of his family. Relations between superiors and subordinates within the bureaucracy may thus be viewed as a logical extension of Egyptian family patterns in which individuals are socialized to accept the absolute authority of the father. Third, Egyptians have been ruled by successive waves of foreign conquerors. Deferential behavior, albeit superficial and mocking, became an essential element in personal survival.

Not all of Egypt's bureaucratic norms, however, find their origins in Egypt's historical traditions. The dramatic expansion of the bureaucracy during the socialist era found many officials holding positions for which they lacked adequate credentials. Such individuals found it expedient to compensate for their lack of qualifications and the inherent vulnerability of their status by deference to superiors, by strict adherence to the rules, and by the avoidance of responsibilities that might reveal their deficiencies. Bureaucratic inflation, to use Nazih Ayubi's term, continued throughout the Sadat era, extending trends initiated during the reign of his predecessor.[20]

Bureaucratic norms were also reinforced by the recruitment policies of the postrevolutionary governments. The welfare orientation of the Nasser era and the concomitant graduates policy made bureaucratic positions a right of graduates, a fiefdom to which they were entitled by virtue of their university degree. Neither the obtaining of a bureaucratic position nor job security once in that position were pegged to performance or to public service. One of the questionnaire items in the Al Ahram survey, by way of illustration, asked our respondents to indicate what their friends and relatives had advised them were the major advantages of a bureaucratic career prior to their entrance into government service. The results provided in table 2.1, speak for themselves. The vast majority of our respondents entered the bureaucracy predisposed to apathy.

By way of background, it should be noted that it is possible to enter government service by various means, the most prominent of which are merit examinations, graduates policy, and *wasta* (influence). Applicants seeking to enter government service via graduation from Egyptian universities or high schools (lower-level positions) must wait until the Ministry of Labor announces positions are available for members of their specific graduating class. This process often takes three years or more. Employment opportunities for 1988 graduates, for example, probably will not be announced until 1991, or perhaps later. The Ministry of Labor then assigns applicants to positions throughout the country by a process that is haphazard at best.

Applicants may circumvent the graduates policy by passing examinations conducted independent of the Ministry of Labor by various ministries and public corporations. *Wasta* or influence circumvents both the graduates policy and the examination process. As indicated in Table 2.2, the respondents in the Al Ahram survey represented all three major categories, with graduates predominating. Later sections of the analysis will examine the impact of recruitment on performance.

The above observations concerning the origins of bureaucratic culture are applicable both to the mainline bureaucratic units and to

Table 2.1

Advantages of a Bureaucratic Career*
(n = 637; nonresponse = 2)

When your friends and relatives discussed government service, what were the advantages they talked about?

1.	Low hours	17.0%
2.	Minimal responsibility	5.3
3.	Steady income	25.7
4.	Easy work	8.3
5.	Permanent	25.1
6.	Good vacations	1.1
7.	Low competition	1.1
8.	Prestige	2.4
9.	No obligations	12.9
10.	Other	1.1
		100%

*Only lower- and middle-level respondents were asked this question.

the public sector. It should be noted, however, that the public sector was created by the Nasser regime and bore the full brunt of socialist recruitment and welfare policies. In this regard, Samir Youssef argues that Egypt entered the socialist era almost totally lacking a professional managerial class capable of effectively managing public sector enterprises. Starting with the works of Max Weber, Youssef argues that enterprises in the capitalist societies of the West evolved from individual proprietorships or small partnerships dominated by the owners or partners into large public (or private) corporations operated by professional managers external to the ownership group. This process was accompanied by changes in the psychology and skills of the professional managers, the most pronounced of which was the evolution from paternalism to the impersonal accountability of managerial performance based upon profits. This evolution, he argues, had yet to occur with the advent of socialism in Egypt. The man-

Table 2.2

*Method of Recruitment**
(n = 632; nonresponse = 7)

Which of the following was most important in securing your position in government service?

1. Graduates policy	41.3%	
2. *Wasta* (influence)	10.3	
3. Normal channels	44.6	
4. Other	3.8	
	100%	

*This question was limited to lower- and middle-level respondents.

agerial pool available to Egypt was predominantly "patriarchal." Managers viewed the firms they managed as an extension of their families.[24] Youssef also notes that the rapid expansion of the industrial sector rapidly exhausted the existing pool of managers, forcing the government to draw heavily upon the military and the mainline bureaucrats to fill available positions. This is an important point, inasmuch as it forged an important link between the mainline bureaucratic units and the public sector corporations.

Youssef also seconds an earlier analysis of Egyptian culture by Saad Eddin Ibrahim, suggesting that the Egyptian work culture was beset by submissiveness, fatalism, particularism, a lack of teamwork, a rigidity of class attitudes, familism, and technological dependency on the West.[25] The later point focuses on the lack of indigenous technological innovation. Youssef concludes his analysis of managerial (and work) culture in Egypt by suggesting:

> Just after the revolution, during the waves of nationalization, political loyalty was an important selection criterion. While it is logical to expect that Egyptian managers have become more professional as they have gained more experience, available data also suggest that they are not highly professional in the application of scientific method to their work. It is still possible that the background of

most top Egyptian managers has exerted considerable influence on younger second line managers. It has been found, for example, that older managers and board members, as well as those who began their careers in government, are noticeably political in their behavior.[26]

Reinforcement of Bureaucratic Culture in Egypt

Egyptian bureaucratic culture appears to be reinforced by a variety of factors. To begin with, many of the forces that originally shaped Egypt's bureaucratic culture remain operative. The list of such continuing factors would certainly include the graduates policy, the low salary levels, the ironclad job security and most of the structural and environmental problems outlined earlier.

Second, one could well argue that the sense of relative (and real) deprivation resulting from the growing disparity in the wage structures of the government and the private sectors has reinforced existing cultural norms by creating a crisis in bureaucratic morale. The new wealth of the private sector has also tarnished the traditional prestige of the bureaucracy, a circumstance evidenced by the recent tendency of bureaucratic families to make marriage alliances with the private sector rather than within the government sector. On the positive side, of course, the *infitah* has also made it easier for government officials to find second jobs.

Third, the bureaucracy is under attack from all sides: the political system, the public, the private sector, and the international sector represented by the International Monetary Fund and USAID. It has been forced into a position of retrenchment, of defense. It is fighting to retain what it has rather than looking toward the future.

Objectives and Methodology

The above portrayal of the Egyptian bureaucracy was based largely upon participant observation and informal interviews with a wide variety of Egyptian scholars and officials. It also drew upon observations in the Egyptian press as well as a wide variety of published works and Ph.D. dissertations.

The task of the Al Ahram project was to go beyond impressionistic data and to provide an empirical assessment of levels of drive, flexibility, innovation, and mass rapport within the government sector. Additionally, the Al Ahram project sought to examine the underpinnings of the behavioral variables in question and to suggest ways that levels of drive, flexibility, innovation, and mass regarding might be increased within the Egyptian context. Again, we would stress that assessment is the logical starting point of reform. Merely "knowing" that problems exist is not an adequate substitute for empirical assessments of the nature, severity, and variation of the problem areas. Some areas and strata of the bureaucracy function much better than others. The objective of our research was to identify the good as well as the bad, to suggest ways in which the bureaucratic process in Egypt could draw upon its own experience.

The data presented previously are based largely upon a survey of 826 Egyptian civil servants conducted by the Al Ahram Center for Strategic and Political Studies during the late spring of 1983. The sample was selected in fairly equal proportions from three government sector agencies: the Ministry of Social Affairs (n = 252), the Ministry of Industry (n = 272), and the Aluminum Corporation (n = 271). The three administrative agencies represent a service-oriented bureaucracy, a production-oriented bureaucracy, and an on-line public sector bureaucracy. The Aluminum Corporation was selected because of its reputation as one of the most productive of Egypt's public sector companies, thereby providing an opportunity to examine the bureaucratic process in what is reputed to be one of Egypt's best-run bureaucracies. The sample was stratified to reflect the senior (n = 156), middle-management (n = 321), and lower levels (n = 319) of the Egyptian bureaucracy. Within stratified categories, respondents were selected randomly from employment records. The questionnaires were administered in person by a specially trained team of sociology graduate students from Ein Shams University in Cairo.

The questionnaire was designed in the Arabic language by a five-member team of researchers at the center. The original questionnaire was pretested using a pretest sample of seventy officials reflecting all employment levels. The questionnaire averaged approximately 130 items in length, with separate versions of the questionnaire being administered to each of the three administrative levels. Approximately 75 percent of the questionnaire items were uniform across the three levels, with the remaining 25 percent of the items being tailored to the unique characteristics of each level. The questionnaires were administered as direct interviews and resulted in a response rate of 100 percent. Thirty questionnaires were deleted from the sample as a result of excessive nonresponses or technical problems.

The reliability of the questionnaire was ascertained by comparing response patterns among similar items as well as by matching response patterns with well-established characteristics of the bureaucracy. The level of contradictory responses among the matched items was less than 4 percent with little discernible evidence of response bias among similar items with inverted response selections.[27]

The Al Ahram study also drew upon a wide variety of government reports, Ph.D. dissertations, press reports, and personal interviews. We would also be less than candid if we did not acknowledge the experience and participant observation of members of the research team.

Some Limitations of the Study

Because of the broad scope of the Al Ahram study, it is important to note its limitations. First, the study is concerned with those behavioral dimensions of bureaucratic behavior that have an overall influence upon the capacity of the Egyptian bureaucracy to play a dynamic role in the developmental process. The study was not designed as a time and motion analysis of how specific bureaucrats perform their daily functions. Such analyses are important but exceed the scope of the present study.

Second, the majority of the data presented in the present volume are based upon survey research. The advantage of survey research is that it provides researchers with the means to study the attitudes and behavior of a large number of individuals in a short period of time. The disadvantage of survey research is that the information garnered is narrow in scope. Survey research also provides but a snapshot of attitudes and behavior at one point in time. The data presented in the Al Ahram study, accordingly, is meant to be used in conjunction with a variety of other data sources readily available to students of Egyptian bureaucracy. Such other sources would surely include the works of Ayubi, Berger, Youssef, and Muna.[28]

Third, the Al Ahram study is concerned with assessing the behavior of Egyptian officials. By necessity, assessing human behavior often involves assessing the attitudes and opinions of the respondents. As the reader will observe, many of the questionnaire items employed in the Al Ahram study are attitudinal in nature. While attitudes and opinions are important in their own right, the link between attitudes and overt behavior is far from absolute and is influenced by a wide variety of psychological and environmental variables.

Format

The objective of the present chapter has been to provide a general picture of the Egyptian bureaucracy, its history, its problems, and its political, social, and economic milieus. Chapters 2 through 7 address and evaluate the developmental capacity of the Egyptian bureaucracy in terms of drive, flexibility, innovation, and mass rapport. Finally, chapter 8 addresses the major conclusions and recommendations of the study.

3

Apathy, Values, Incentives, and Development

The major economic problem facing Egypt today, according to recent speeches by President Mubarak, is apathy. If Egyptians would work harder and produce more, President Mubarak contends, the Egyptian economy could rid itself of oppressive trade deficits and play its logical role as the industrial hub of the Arab world.[1] President Mubarak's views have found strong support in the Egyptian press. A recent critique of the Egyptian productivity in the popular Egyptian weekly magazine *Rose-Al Youssef*, for example, scorned "the feeble productivity of Egyptian workers in most areas of endeavor," citing the bureaucracy as being a place "where everyone is seeking gain without effort . . . a situation that placed thousands of parasites on the surface of Egyptian society."[2]

Bureaucracy, Productivity, and Incentives

The burden of increasing productivity within the Egyptian economy is, in essence, the burden of increasing productivity within the Egyptian bureaucracy. Since the advent of the "socialist laws" of 1961, the Egyptian bureaucracy has been the predominant force in the Egyptian economy, both planning and coordinating the economic policies of the state and operating Egypt's major industrial organiza-

An earlier version of this chapter appeared in the Summer 1985 issue of *The Middle East Journal* (vol. 39, no. 3, pp. 341–61). The present chapter includes data and analysis not part of the earlier article.

tions. The emergence of a revitalized private sector in the *infitah* or open door era of President Sadat did not radically alter this picture, for the private sector is primarily engaged in service, construction, tourist, and real estate activities. The industrial sector of the economy, with minor exceptions, continues to be planned, operated, and regulated by the bureaucracy.

As a first step toward increasing the productivity of the Egyptian bureaucracy, including the public sector corporations that dominate the Egyptian economy, Egyptian policy makers have instituted a variety of incentive systems designed to reward enhanced performance. An employee's income is now based upon a complex mixture of base pay, allowances, and incentives. As President Mubarak has indicated, however, the current system of incentives fails to distinguish between productive and nonproductive workers. Incentives, as presently constituted, have frequently become an integral part of the salary structure and are incentives in name only.

One might question, however, whether monetary incentives will serve as the expected panacea for Egypt's productive ills. While monetary incentives have increased productivity under certain circumstances, it is not at all certain that those circumstances are or can be duplicated in Egypt.[3] In this regard, several factors must be considered. First, it is doubtful that low productivity is merely the result of laziness or apathy among Egyptian workers. Other problems limiting the productivity of government employees in Egypt would certainly include overstaffing, duplication of functions, poorly defined responsibilities, excessive centralization, and various other structural and environmental factors discussed in chapters 1 and 2.[4] The presence of these and related factors makes it difficult for many employees to work effectively even if they are so inclined. Incentives cannot solve what are inherently structural or systemic problems.

Second, adding further monetary incentives would be extremely costly and may not be economically feasible. Not only would an ambitious monetary incentive program strain limited government revenues, but it would also compete with intense pressures to provide across-the-board increases in government salaries. The pressures for across-the-board increases stem from the exceptionally low levels of government salaries, from the growing disparity between salaries in the public sector and the corresponding salaries in the private sector, and from the probability that the government will be forced to modify if not abolish the price supports and subsidies that make existing bureaucratic salaries tenable. Moreover, it is doubtful that the govermnent would be able to reallocate existing incentive programs in a manner that would enable it to reward productive workers at the expense of their less-productive colleagues. Incentives have already become part of the salary base. A redistribution of existing incentives, accordingly, would push many employees below the subsistence level, wreaking havoc with bureaucratic morale and creating political tensions. If the government cannot afford both to increase monetary incentives and to provide a general increase in government salaries, it may find it politically expedient to stress across-the-board increases. It could also be argued that improving overall salary levels is an essential step in alleviating obstacles to bureaucratic productivity. As data to be presented shortly indicate, current salary levels force most government employees to seek supplemental income and do depress productivity levels.

Third, one must consider the social ramifications of an incentive system that would make the salaries of some but not all government employees equivalent to corresponding salaries in the private sector. The prevailing ideology of Egypt is still one of social equality. Indeed, one of the fundamental reasons for the awesome size of the Egyptian bureaucracy has been the government's desire to provide all citizens and particularly university graduates with a position in the bureaucracy as a means of achieving full employment. Dramatic imbalances in salary levels would inevitably create conflict within the bureaucracy and would, in all probability, have political repercussions as well.

Finally, one must question whether the institution of monetary incentives as a means of increasing worker productivity was based upon a thorough study of the values of Egyptian bureaucrats or whether it was instituted intuitively as an easy solution to the problem. We raise this question because the recognized benefits of government employment in Egypt are security, stability, and perhaps, prestige. Nonmonetary incentives or a combination of monetary and nonmonetary incentives might well prove to be a more feasible means of improving productivity than monetary incentives alone. This, at least, has been the conclusion of extensive management studies in the United States and Western Europe.[5]

Within the context of the above discussion, the objectives of the present chapter are (1) to assess the magnitude of the apathy problem within the Egyptian bureaucracy, (2) to explore the various reasons for the existence of the apathy problem to the extent that it does, indeed, exist, (3) to examine the incentive values of Egyptian bureaucrats in a comparative and theoretical perspective, and (4) to suggest possible alternative or supplementary incentives that might be used in place of or in addition to monetary incentives as a means of increasing the productivity of government employees.

Results: Assessing Low Productivity

Assessing bureaucratic productivity is a difficult and subjective task under the best of circumstances. It is a particularly difficult task in Egypt and the Middle East. In the course of our research, for example, the Al Ahram Center was unsuccessful in its attempts to ascertain precisely how the Ministry of Industry distinguished its most productive units from its least productive units. If such an ordering mechanism exists, it certainly was not disclosed. The Aluminum Corporation, as noted above, was included in the study on the basis of its reputation as one of Egypt's premier public sector enterprises.

In the absence of alternative sources of information, our evaluations of productivity within the Egyptian bureaucracy were necessarily limited to survey data. This is an unfortunate limitation inasmuch as individuals tend to be inaccurate in evaluating their own performance levels. It is also unrealistic to ask people to incriminate themselves by acknowledging low levels of performance.

In an effort to mitigate the above limitations, the study employed five diverse measures of productivity. The first was an assessment by senior-level bureaucrats of the productivity levels of their subordinates. This is an important measure of productivity inasmuch as senior bureaucrats are responsible by law for evaluating the productivity of their subordinates. They should know. The results of this stage of the analysis are presented in Table 3.1.

Our second measure of productivity was based upon two items contained in a sixteen-item group dynamics scale in which middle- and lower-level bureaucrats were asked to describe the work environment in which they operated. Specifically, respondents were asked to respond to two Likert scale items suggesting (1) that most of their peers worked hard and (2) that most of their peers were lazy. Al-

Table 3.1

Assessments of Low Productivity among Egyptian Bureaucrats by Senior Officials
(n = 156; nonresponse = 8)

What percentage of your subordinates normally put in a hard day's work?

Percent	Total	Aluminum	Industry	Social
0–10	10.3	2	12.8	15.5
11–21	9.7	8	10.6	10.3
21–40	20.6	14	23.4	24.1
41–60	41.3	42	42.6	39.7
61–100	18.1	34	10.6	10.3
	100%*	100%	100%	100%

*Totals may vary from 100% owing to rounding error.

though the two items did not ask the respondents to criticize themselves, they did ask for candid evaluations of peers, evaluations that some respondents may have been reluctant to make. We would note, however, that the two items received very similar results in spite of the fact that they were worded in inverse order and appeared at alternate ends of the group dynamics scale. The text and results of the group dynamics scale are presented in Table 3.2.

The third measure of productivity was based upon sources of professional information. In this regard, it was assumed that individuals who took the time and effort to consult professional materials in the execution of their job responsibilities would be more productive than individuals who relied upon other members of the work unit for their professional information.[6] The percentage distributions are provided in Table 3.3. The professional-reference measure of productivity was probably more accurate in assessing the productivity of middle- and upper-level officials than it was the productivity of lower-level officials in as much as many of the lower-level positions do not require advanced skills.

The fourth indicator of productivity was based upon the work-value index to be discussed shortly (Table 3.7) and distinguishes

Table 3.2

Group Dynamics Scale
(Middle- and Lower-Level Respondents)

Sometimes an administrator's ability to achieve his objectives is influenced by his work environment. In this regard, please evaluate the individuals you work with by indicating whether you (strongly agree, agree, disagree, or strongly disagree) with the following statements.

	Weighted Score	Strongly Agree Scores %
1. Work hard	60	28.6
2. Accept new ideas	39	9.3
3. Open and honest with each other	48	18.0
4. Accept new responsibility easily	43	14.4
5. *Delegate authority frequently	29	5.7
6. Treat public with respect	57	26.5
7. *Responsive to constructive criticism	36	8.5
8. *Public service over job security	26	4.5
9. *Willing to accept conflict	15	5.1
10. *Are not lazy	64	41.7
11. Impartial toward friends and relatives	25	8.9
12. Decisive	38	10.4
13. *Willing to take risks	28	7.9
14. *Flexible in executing decisions	28	6.5
15. Listen to public opinions	43	9.3
16. Solicit public opinions	31	8.9

Key: Low scores indicate problem severity.

*In order to assess problems of response bias some of the questionnaire items in this section were presented in a positive format while others were presented in a negative format. Asterisks indicate items presented in a negative format in the questionnaire, i.e., "are not lazy" was presented as "are lazy." All questions are presented in a positive format in the table to facilitate comparison of the scores.

**The scale scores range between 0 and 100 and represent summarized scores of Likert scale items (strongly agree, agree, disagree, strongly disagree) in which "strongly agree" responses have been given twice the weight of "agree" responses. Weighted scores of 30 or less indicate severe problem areas.

Table 3.3

Measures of Bureaucratic Productivity

Value-Based Productivity (middle and lower levels only)

high	13.3
medium	41.8
low	44.8
	100%* (n = 640, nonresponse = 8)

Professional-Reference Productivity (all levels)

high	8.6
medium	34.6
low	56.9
	100% (n = 796, nonresponse = 0)

Job-Satisfaction Productivity (all levels)

high	30.1
low	69.9
	100% (n = 796, nonresponse = 14)

*Totals may vary from 100% owing to rounding error.

between individuals who placed greater and lesser emphasis upon job comfort and job security.[7] Individuals primarily concerned with the comfort and security of their positions were judged to be less productive than individuals willing to expend greater effort for the sake of money or prestige. This indicator of productivity is applicable only to the lower and middle levels of the bureaucracy.

The final and most important measure of productivity was based upon open-ended questionnaire items requesting respondents at all levels to indicate the things they liked most about their jobs. The responses were then grouped into productive and nonproductive categories, the text and percentage distributions for which appear in Table 3.4. The assumption of this particular measure of productivity was that individuals who were upset by low salaries or transportation problems or who found social relations to be the most pleasing aspect of their job would be less productive than individuals listing work-

Table 3.4

Job Satisfaction and Dissatisfaction
Job Dissatisfaction
(n = 796; nonresponse = 48)

Herzberg Category	Egyptian Response Categories	Egypt	Herzberg	British	Egypt	Herzberg	British
Achievement	effort to improve work, moral incentive			8.9	3.7		23.4
Growth	appreciation of boss,			1.7	4.1		1.0
Recognition	work directly with boss,			4.2	5.4		4.5
Responsibility	democratic decision making, free expression of views			8.7			20.0
Work Itself	lack of specialists, excessive routine, match of skills with job, division of labor, quality of information funding	26.9		32.8	16.9		39.7
Advancement	lack of incentives	1.7					
		28.6%	31%	56.3%	30.1%	81%	88.6%
Policy and Administration	democratic administration			13.7	1.0		
Supervision	lack of clout	3.5		20.3			1.2

Motivators

52

Relations with Supervisor	partiality of boss, boss oppressive, boss lacks confidence, evaluations	5.4			8.5		
Work Conditions	transportation, cleanliness, scheduling of hours, lack of tension, peace and quiet	11.1	2.5		7.1		4.4
Salary	salary	43.9	2.3				0.7
Relationship with Peers	sloppiness of work, peer workers, cooperation with peers, social relations	3.6	5.0		50.9		5.1
Personal life	pressure of external works, impact of work on family	4.0					
Relationships with Subordinates							
Status							
Security							
Alienation					2.4		
		71.5	69	43.8	69.9	19	11.4
		100%	100%	100%	100%	100%	100%

Hygiene

related concerns such as the ability to use their specialization or the appreciation of their supervisor.

The job satisfaction/dissatisfaction measure of productivity was based directly upon the work of Frederick Herzberg. Herzberg's theory of productivity was based upon a detailed analysis of the sources of job satisfaction and job dissatisfaction in twelve diverse studies with a combined sample of 1,685. The respondents "included lower-level supervisors, professional women, agricultural administrators, men about to retire from management positions, hospital maintenance personnel, manufacturing supervisors, nurses, food handlers, military officers, engineers, scientists, housekeepers, teachers, technicians, female assemblers, accountants, Finnish foremen and Hungarian engineers."[8]

As a result of his analysis of this extensive and varied data set, Herzberg concluded that employees responded to two diverse stimuli: hygienic stimuli and motivational stimuli. Hygienic stimuli include salary structure, work conditions, and security. Motivational stimuli, by contrast, focused upon opportunities for achievement, recognition, and growth. Hygienic stimuli were negative stimuli and were the basis of job dissatisfaction. As such, they were the source of complaints and tended to depress performance if they fell below reasonable levels. Their role as motivators was basically a negative one of pain avoidance. Once satisfactory hygienic conditions were reached, their motivational role decreased.

Herzberg's "motivators," by contrast, were positive stimuli. As they caused little direct pain or personal inconvenience, they were infrequently cited as the primary source of job dissatisfaction. By building upon the need for recognition and growth, however, they provided positive stimuli for increasing production.

Within the context of assessing the productivity of the Egyptian bureaucracy, Herzberg's theory suggests that job satisfaction should emerge as a better indicator of productivity than job dissatisfaction. This hypothesis, if sustained, is critical to future bureaucratic reform efforts, for it suggests that merely improving salaries or other "hygienic" structural and environmental conditions will be of minimal utility in increasing bureaucratic productivity. This theme will be examined at various points within the present chapter. It will also form a central theme in the multivariate analyses presented in chapter 7.

Turning to the first measure of productivity, the sample of

senior bureaucrats was requested to indicate the approximate percentage of their subordinates who "put in a hard day's work." The results,
presented in Table 3.1, indicate that the overwhelming majority of the
senior bureaucrats surveyed felt that most of their subordinates were
not putting in a hard day's work. Ten percent of the respondents
suggested that almost none of their subordinates were particularly
productive. The assessments of the senior bureaucrats, then, support
President Mubarak's contention that low worker productivity is one
of the major ills besetting the Egyptian economy.

In striking contrast to the senior evaluations, the peer evaluations, presented in the context of the group dynamics scale (Table
3.2), indicate that apathy is the least of the problems that beset the
Egyptian bureaucracy. The composite scores for each item listed in
Table 3.2 range from 0 to 100, with scores over 50 indicating at least
adequate work performance and scores of 30 or less indicating problems of extreme severity.[9]

The composite scores presented in Table 3.2 indicate that mid-
dle- and lower-level bureaucrats do not perceive worker apathy to be
a major detriment to bureaucratic performance. Moreover, it is difficult to dismiss their apathy evaluations merely as an artifact of their
reluctance to criticize their peers, for their response patterns clearly
distinguished between the six dimensions of bureaucratic behavior
measured by the group dynamics scale. Particularly noteworthy is the
score of 25 for *wasta* or the granting of favors to friends and relatives,
an issue of extreme sensitivity in Egypt and one that respondents
would clearly avoid if they were making a concerted effort to shape
their answers.

How, then, does one explain the conflicting evaluations of the
senior bureaucrats on one hand, and those of the middle- and lower-
level bureaucrats on the other? The answer, in the view of the research
team, lies in the fact that most Egyptians perceive themselves as being
willing to work if work is available. Work, however, may seldom be
available in accessible form. Overstaffing, random appointment,
poorly defined responsibilities, multiple clearances, and over-
centralization, to mention but a few problems besetting the Egyptian
bureaucracy, often mean that officials may spend long periods of time
waiting for work to appear. The low wages provided by the Egyptian
government provide little incentive for seeking work. Moreover, as
the low peer scores on the "conflict," "risk taking," and the "flexible
execution of orders" items on Table 3.2 indicate, little group pressure

exists to generate work by sticking one's neck out and minding other people's business.

A particularly dramatic illustration distinguishing between the willingness to do work and the lesser willingness to seek work is provided by responses to two related questionnaire items which addressed the *need* for organizational change and the *desire* for organizational change. When asked if organizational changes were essential to improve the performance of their units, 87 percent of the respondents answered in the affirmative. When asked at an earlier point if they had ever become so upset by existing rules and regulations that they really wanted to change them, 86 percent of the respondents indicated either little (44 percent) or no (43 percent) desire for change.

Finally, one must note that apathy, hard work, and laziness are relative terms. One is either productive or nonproductive in comparison to the behavior or norms of a group. What the peer evaluations suggest in the final analysis is that middle- and lower-level bureaucrats are willing to work within the organizational context in which they find themselves. They will do the work that is placed before them. They are reluctant, however, to alter or to go beyond that organizational context. Inasmuch as the organizational procedures, environmental circumstances, and cultural norms of the bureaucracy are all stacked against greater productivity, there is little in the milieu of the Egyptian bureaucrats to motivate them to become a productive force in Egypt's development.

The assessments of the senior officials and the peer evaluations were reinforced by both the professional-reference and the work-value indicators of productivity. In regard to the work-value measure, 44.8 percent of the middle- and lower-level respondents stressed job comfort and job ease as important work values. Forty-one percent of the respondents listed either job comfort or job ease as an important value, and only 13 percent did not mention job ease or job comfort as a work value. The work-value percentages are summarized in Table 3.3. The broader results from which these percentages have been drawn are provided in Table 3.7.

The professional-reference indicator of productivity produced similar percentage distributions, indicating that 56 percent of the respondents were not inclined to consult professional materials in the execution of the responsibilities. Approximately 34 percent of the respondents consulted professional materials on an occasional basis, with approximately 9 percent of the respondents indicating that professional materials provided an important source of job-related information. The results of the professional-reference indicator of productivity are also presented in Table 3.3.

Turning to the final indicator of productivity, the respondent's listing of the things they liked least and most about their positions is presented in Table 3.4. The responses have been grouped to correspond to Herzberg's categories. As such they provide a basis for testing Herzberg's theory and for comparing the Egyptian data with a parallel cross-national data. The cross-national comparisons are particularly important inasmuch as the job-satisfaction/dissatisfaction data represent the only area of the Al Ahram data for which cross-national norms are available.

By far and away the most important source of job dissatisfaction among the respondents was low salary, a hygienic rather than a motivational concern. The picture is similar in regard to the "like most" item. In this case "social relations" topped the list of preferred items, more than doubling the score of the most preferred production-related item, that being the match between skill and position.

In order to place the Egyptian data in perspective, it is necessary to examine the hypothesis that productivity is lower in Egypt than it is in the bureaucracies of the West. It is also necessary to test the hypothesis that job satisfaction is a better indicator of productivity than job dissatisfaction.

Comparative data relating to the cross-national sources of job satisfaction and job dissatisfaction are provided by Herzberg. Parallel data for Britain are provided by Livingstone and Wilkie's test of Herzberg's theory among a sample of 464 British civil servants.[10] In terms of the sources of job dissatisfaction, one finds little difference between the Egyptian responses and the responses reported by Herzberg. The British responses, while more productivity oriented than the Egyptian responses, were biased by the fact that the British civil servants had received a substantial raise in salary just prior to the study. All in all, then, the sources and levels of job dissatisfaction among Egyptian bureaucrats were not divergent from Western norms.

When the sources and levels of job satisfaction among Egyptian bureaucrats are compared with their Western counterparts, by contrast, the differences are staggering. Only 30 percent of the Egyptian respondents emphasized productivity-related sources or job satisfaction as opposed to 81 percent of the Herzberg samples and 88 percent of the British sample. In terms of the job-satisfaction indicator of productivity, then, Egyptian civil servants are drastically below the productivity norms of England and the various Western states included in Herzberg's analysis.

This brings us to the critical test of Herzberg's hypothesis. Is job satisfaction a better indicator of productivity than job dissatisfaction within the Egyptian context? This question is critical to bureaucratic reform in Egypt, for if sources of dissatisfaction are unrelated to productivity, it is unlikely that systemic improvements such as across-the-board raises will produce the increases in productivity so ardently sought by President Mubarak.

If job satisfaction is to be judged a better indicator of productivity among Egyptian officials than job dissatisfaction, two conditions should be met. First, the job-satisfaction indicator should correlate positively with professional-reference and work-value indicators of productivity. Second the job-dissatisfaction indicator should not be correlated with the professional-reference and work-value indicators of productivity (or should correate negatively therewith.) The peer and supervisor evaluations were indirect measures of productivity and could not be used to test the hypothesis.

The gamma coefficient for the cross tabulations between the job-satisfaction indicator of productivity and the professional-reference indicator of productivity was (g = .231).[11] The coefficient strengthened when controlled for job level, being stronger among middle- (g = .262) and upper- (g = .276) level respondents, but insignificant among lower-level respondents.[12] This variation by job level reflects the anticipated probability that many lower-level officials may not find professional references appropriate for the positions. The coefficients for the middle and upper-level officials were (g = .262) and (g = .276), respectively. Job dissatisfaction was unrelated to the professional-reference indicator of productivity at any level. Indeed, there was some suggestion that it was negatively related to productivity.

Cross tabulations between the job-satisfaction and the work-value indicator of productivity indicated that the two variables were positively correlated but only minimally so (g = .158). The picture changes, however, when the correlations are controlled for job level. The work-value indicator of productivity correlates with job satisfaction among the middle-level bureaucrats (g = .236) and is unrelated to productivity among lower level bureaucrats. The job-dissatisfaction indicator, again, was unrelated to the work-valued measure of productivity at any level.

In light of the data's support for the Herzberg hypothesis, one may conclude that job satisfaction is a valid indicator of productivity among Egyptian officials, particularly officials at the middle and upper levels. Equally important, the data make it quite clear that job dissatisfaction is not related to productivity. This point will have a direct influence on the subsequent discussions of incentives. Finally, one is also forced to accept the conclusion that the production levels of Egyptian bureaucrats are woefully below international norms.

Explanations of Apathy

In an effort to come to grips with the causes of low productivity among Egyptian bureaucrats as well as to obtain a more complete picture of Egypt's bureaucratic problems in general, our sample of senior officials was requested to evaluate the importance of various reasons generally offered to explain the low productivity of Egyptian bureaucrats. The most prominent reasons offered in explanation of the low productivity of Egyptian bureaucrats are provided in Table 3.5, as are weighted summary scores indicating the relative importance of each item. As in the case of the summary scores presented in earlier stages of the analysis, the scores range between 0 and 100. Items receiving scores of 50 or above should be considered important contributors to the low productivity of Egyptian bureaucrats.

The data presented in Table 3.5 indicate that the problem of low productivity, in addition to the inadequacy of incentives, is a multifaceted one involving a variety of organizational, cultural, group dynamic, and supervisor-related dimensions. A quick fix, accordingly, may be difficult to come by.

In addition to the variables outlined in Table 3.5, explanations of the low productivity of Egyptian bureaucrats are also to be found in both the recruitment practices of the Egyptian bureaucracy and in the dire economic circumstance of the average bureaucrat. In regard to recruitment, it was noted earlier that bureaucratic recruitment in Egypt gives preference to full employment over the building of an efficient bureaucratic organization. Most Egyptian officials attained their position through one of three ways: routine appointment of

Table 3.5

*Some Explanations of Low Productivity among Egyptian Bureaucrats
by Senior Officials*
(n = 156)

Explanations of Low Productivity	Weighted Scores	Very Important Scores Only
1. Systemic		
Inadequate skills	55	43.3
Low incentives	79	59.5
Responsibility not clear	46	27.0
Inadequate penalties	64	41.8
2. Cultural/Personal		
Low concern for responsibilities	42	19.7
Social responsibilities	55	36.4
3. Group Dynamics		
No one else works hard	52	30.5
4. Supervisor Dynamics		
Lack of reinforcement	51	25.0

Key: High scores reflect problem areas.

*Each of the senior respondents was requested to evaluate each of the items summarized above as being "very important," "important," "minimally important," or "unimportant" as an explanation of apathy in their respective units. Scale scores range from 0 to 100 with "very important" responses receiving twice the weight of "important" responses. Responses of minimal or no importance were not included in the calculations. Scores in excess of 50 should be considered major problems.

university graduates, competitive examination, or *wasta* (favoritism). In the case of routine appointments of graduates, applicants may have waited up to three or four years following their graduation from college for their appointment to materialize. Of the middle- and lower-level respondents in our sample, 41 percent received their appointments via graduation, 45 percent by competitive examination, and 11 percent by *wasta*. The remaining 3 percent did not respond to the question. Given this breakdown, we hypothesized that those who entered the bureaucracy via competitive examinations or merit might possibly be more productive than officials who entered the bureaucracy through noncompetitive channels. This, however, did not prove to be the case.

Perhaps more detrimental to individual productivity than the avenue of recruitment were the perceptions of the Egyptian civil servants upon entering government service. For instance, when respondents were asked what their friends and relatives felt to be the major advantages of government service, the list was headed by "permanent," 25 percent; "firm income," 25 percent; "low hours," 17 percent; "no obligations," 12 percent; "easy," 8 percent; and "low responsibility," 5 percent. Quite clearly, then, the primary lure of government service is security, hardly a quality to be associated with dynamic productivity.

Turning to the impact of the dire economic circumstances of the average Egyptian bureaucrat upon bureaucratic productivity, it must be recalled that during the Nasser era Egypt was transformed into a socialist state with salaries and promotion procedures being tightly regulated by the government. Salaries were remarkably low by world standards, but the range between high and low salaries was narrow and most government employees played by more or less the same financial rules. During the Sadat era, the *infitah* or open door policy revitalized Egypt's private sector, contributing to spiraling inflation and a widening gap between the wages of the private sector and those of the public sector. Government salaries, if minimally adequate under Nasser, became wholly inadequate under Sadat. Government employees, while legally prohibited from holding second jobs, found extra employment an economic necessity. Eighty-nine percent of our respondents, for example, acknowledged holding second jobs with 84 percent of those respondents holding second jobs working between three and five hours per day in their supplemental positions.

While holding a second job does not automatically preclude high productivity, it does suggest that the individual's energies are being spread very thin. The fact that government jobs are prized for security rather than income also suggests that whatever productive energies the individual may possess are likely to be saved for their private sector positions—positions in which such energies are more likely to be rewarded. The high percentage of respondents holding second jobs also may explain why bureaucrats do not perceive themselves as lazy.

The economic strain on Egyptian bureaucrats is also evidenced by the thousands of civil servants who leave the bureaucracy annually to work in either the public sector or in the oil-producing states. Thirty-five percent of our respondents, for example, were seriously contemplating a move to either the Gulf or to the private sector. An additional 32 percent of the respondents acknowledged giving considerable thought to such a move. Under such circumstances, commitment to their present positions can hardly be strong. Indeed, senior officials often complain of the difficulty of retaining their best people. Our data reflected this trend with those individuals ranking high in terms of productivity being somewhat more likely to consider moving to the private sector or to the Gulf than their less-productive colleagues (G = .244).

The role of low salaries in depressing productivity, then, goes far beyond the lowering of employee morale or the creation of an atmosphere in which employees feel that the lowness of their wages does not warrant extra effort. Low wages add to the physical and psychological stress of the employee by necessitating external employment. They also result in high levels of turnover in skilled positions.

Finally, it must again be stressed that low productivity in the Egyptian bureaucracy involves a variety of organizational problems in addition to the behavioral or motivational problems surveyed above. This fact is manifest in responses by senior bureaucrats to a questionnaire item requesting them to indicate what they believed to be the major obstacles to the efficient operation of the Egyptian bureaucracy. The scores provided in Table 3.6 indicate that the single major problem facing the Egyptian bureaucracy according to the senior bureaucrats sampled, far in advance of the motivational problems relating to salaries and incentives, is red tape.

In summary, then, the multidimensionality of the productivity problem suggests that major increases in worker productivity are unlikely to be achieved overnight, and that dramatic increases in productivity will ultimately be dependent upon a major revitalization of all phases of the bureaucratic process. Be this as it may, the magnitude of Egypt's economic ills demands that worker productivity be increased. A start has to be made somewhere. Both President

Table 3.6

Senior-Level Perceptions of the Main Problems Reducing the Administrative Effectiveness of the Egyptian Bureaucracy
(n = 156; nonresponse = 0)

In your view, what are the main problems that reduce the efficiency of the Egyptian bureaucracy?

Key: High scores indicate problem areas.

Structural Problems	First Choice Only
Red tape	46.2
Rigid laws	12.5
Low funding	4.5
Recruitment/appointment policies	2.6
Low technical skills	3.8
Behavior-Directed Problems	
Favoritism	13.5
Poor incentives	3.2
Low salaries	12.8
Supervisor unresponsive	1.3
	100%*

*Totals may vary from 100% owing to rounding error.

Mubarak and his senior bureaucrats have pinned their hopes on the improvement of Egypt's system of monetary incentives.

Results: Values and Incentives

Given the emphasis that both President Mubarak and our sample of senior administrators have placed upon monetary incentives as the most feasible means of achieving increased productivity, the analysis moved to an examination of the main motivational values of

Egyptian bureaucrats. The purpose of the analysis was to ascertain (1) if monetary values are the most important motivational values of Egyptian bureaucrats, and (2) whether, given the difficulties of implementing a far-reaching monetary incentive program, alternative non-monetary incentives might be equally if not more effective in increasing productivity. In this regard, both the literature on bureaucracy in the developing areas and our informal interviews with Egyptian bureaucrats suggested that six motivational values were of particular importance to Egyptian bureaucrats: money, prestige, an urban location, proximity to relatives, security, and comfort.[13] To ascertain the relative importance of each value vis-à-vis the others, respondents were presented with a scale of fifteen items, each of which contained a choice between two value statements. They were then requested to choose that statement in each pair that they felt was most important to them personally. The results, presented in Table 3.7, indicate the importance of each value vis-à-vis every other value. The summary scale appearing at the bottom of Table 3.7 indicates the overall ranking of each value on a scale ranging from 0 to 100.

The data presented in Table 3.7 indicate quite dramatically that prestige is the predominant motivational value of Egyptian bureaucrats. Money was second in the overall ordering of motivational values but was positioned a clear 38 points below prestige on the weighted preference index and less than 5 points above its nearest competitors, location and security. Moreover, an analysis of the extent to which the six values varied on the basis of job level, ministry, age, sex, place of birth, and education indicates that prestige, in spite of some variation, maintained its dominant position across all of the control categories examined. Money, on the other hand, was of far greater importance to some groups than others. Particularly striking in this regard was the finding that male workers were overwhelmingly more concerned with money than were their female counterparts (g = .552). Females, in turn, were more concerned with a suitable urban location (g = .330). Middle-level and more highly educated officials were also somewhat more concerned about money than lower-level workers, the latter placing slightly greater emphasis on security and comfort. Also noticeable was the reluctance of Cairines to work in the rural areas regardless of the monetary incentives.

Explanations of the above variations are not difficult to come by.

The lower emphasis of female respondents on money is, in all probability, explained by the greater social or cultural flexibility that accrues
to females holding bureaucratic positions vis-à-vis nonworking
females. In what continues to be a male-dominated society in which
the roles of women are severely restricted by social norms, greater
personal freedom is an important female value. Similarly, the clear
preference of female respondents for an urban location can also find at
least partial explanation in the greater social flexibility of the urban
areas. An additional factor, of course, is the general reluctance of
Cairines in general, male or female, to work in what many consider
to be the culturally stifling environment of rural Egypt. Respondents
from the Aluminum Corporation, an enterprise located in rural
Egypt, by contrast, were minimally concerned about the value of an
urban environment. Respondents born in the rural areas were also less
concerned about locational values than their thoroughly urban counterparts.

The results of this phase of the analysis, then, suggest that
monetary incentives and higher salaries may not be the panacea for
increasing worker productivity that the Egyptian government hoped
that they might be. This is particularly the case in terms of inducing
Egyptians to work in the rural areas, a goal that the Egyptian government finds increasingly important as the population of Cairo approaches 14,000,000 and the city's transportation and service
infrastructure nears collapse.

Resolving Contradictions, Comparative Data, and Theoretical Perspectives

In comparing the job dissatisfaction data provided in Table 3.4
with the motivational data presented in Table 3.7, one is confronted
by an apparent contradiction of some magnitude. Low salaries
emerged as the primary source of job dissatisfaction among Egyptian
bureaucrats while prestige surpassed money as the incentive value
most likely to stimulate improved bureaucratic performance. If salaries are the primary source of bureaucratic dissatisfaction, is it not
logical to assume that monetary incentives should also be the preferred incentive value? This apparent contradiction is reinforced by

Table 3.7

Main Incentive Values of Egyptian Bureaucrats
(Low and Medium Level Only)
(n = 640)

Listed below are several pairs of statements. In each pair, please indicate the statement that most agrees with your preference.

a. A high-paying job with low prestige   6.7%
b. A moderately paying job with high prestige   93.3%

a. A high-paying job away from friends and relatives   49.1
b. A moderately paying job near friends and relatives   50.9

a. A high-paying job in the rural areas   52.3
b. A moderately paying job in a city of your choice   47.7

a. A high-paying job that was very difficult and time
   consuming   74.6
b. A moderately paying job that was not too difficult or
   demanding   25.4

a. A high-paying job that involved a great deal of
   responsibility and risk   60.1
b. A moderately paying job that was very secure   39.9

a. A very prestigious job away from family and friends   85.9
b. A respectable job near family and friends   14.1

a. A very prestigious job that involved a great deal of risk and
   responsibility   82.6
b. A respectable job that was very secure   17.4

a. A very prestigious job that was very difficult and time
   consuming   89.7
b. A respectable job that was not too difficult or demanding   10.3

a. A very prestigious job in a rural area   75.7
b. A respectable job in the city of your choice   24.3

a. A very secure position in the rural areas   45.2
b. A position with risks and complex responsibilities in a city
   of your choice   54.8

a. A very secure position away from friends and relatives   50.2
b. A position with risks and complex responsibilities near
   friends and relatives   49.8

Table 3.7
(continued)

a. A very secure position that was difficult and time consuming	74.0
b. A position of risk and responsibility that was not very difficult	26.0
a. A position of little difficulty away from relatives and friends	72.9
b. A difficult and time-consuming position near friends and relatives	27.1
a. A position of little difficulty in the rural areas	41.8
b. A difficult and time-consuming position in the city	58.2
a. A position near friends and relatives in the rural areas	48.6
b. A position away from friends and relatives in a city of your choice	51.4

Weighted Preference Ordering

(Range 0–100)★

Prestige	88
Money	50
Location	46
Security	45
Relatives	39
Comfort	35

★Preference orderings reflect the mean score of total choices for each value over each competing value, doubled. The scale scores range between 0 and 100.

the mass exodus of Egyptian bureaucrats to the Gulf in search of higher salaries as well as by the frank acknowledgment of 89 percent of our respondents that they augmented their bureaucratic salaries with supplemental positions.

This apparent contradiction between salary as a primary source of dissatisfaction and prestige (or other psychological variables) as a dominant motivational force is not unique to Egypt. The work of Herzberg, it will be recalled from the earlier analysis, concluded that employees responded to two diverse types of stimuli: hygienic stimuli and motivational stimuli. Hygienic stimuli include salary structure, work conditions, and security. Motivational stimuli, by contrast, focused upon opportunities for achievement, recognition, and growth. Hygienic stimuli were negative stimuli and were the basis of job dissatisfaction. As such, they were the most visible source of complaints and tended to depress performance if they fell below reasonable levels. Their role as motivators was basically a negative one of pain avoidance. Once satisfactory hygienic conditions were reached, their motivational role decreased. It is far from certain, according to Herzberg's theory, that increasing monetary incentives will automatically result in increased productivity.

Herzberg's "motivators," by contrast, were positive stimuli. They caused little direct pain or personal inconvenience, and, accordingly, they were infrequently cited as the primary source of job dissatisfaction. By building upon the need for recognition and growth, however, they provided a positive stimuli for increasing production.

A wide variety of cross-cultural data also support the differential role of monetary and psychological variables in the motivation of employees. E. C. Nevis, for example, reports that a survey of 5,000 managers selected from the "Fortune 100" companies in the United States ranked wages third in importance in a hierarchy of managerial values based upon the question: "What's important to you?" Values parallel to Herzberg's positive psychological motivators ranked first, second, and fourth. Comparative data for Chinese graduate students at the Shanghi Institute of Mechanical Engineering (n = 28) ranked money fifth, with psychological values ranking first, second and third.[14] A limited study of civil servants in Nigeria similarly found money to be the main source of bureaucratic job dissatisfaction while simultaneously suggesting on the basis of limited data that prestige was the key motivational factor among Nigerian bureaucrats.[15]

Also, a major study of managerial values in private industry involving a sample of 3,641 managers in fourteen countries found a variety of psychological variables, including prestige, to be major concerns of managers in all of the fourteen countries studied. Moreover, the study found that the desire for recognition values was particularly unfulfilled in India, Argentina, Chili, and Italy, the four states in the study most closely approximating conditions in Egypt. It is interesting to note that the authors of the study assumed money to be of secondary motivational value once monetary requirements had reached minimally satisfactory levels.[16]

Two additional studies, one of senior civil servants in the United States (n = 20,000+) and the other of senior civil servants in Great Britain (n = 464) also stressed the distinction between monetary and psychological factors as motivators. The U.S. study, however, stressed the importance of both monetary and psychological factors as motivators, susggesting that the latter should not be stressed at the expense of the former.[17] The British study by Livingstone and Wilkie represented an explicit attempt to replicate Herzberg's work among British civil servants and found involvement in the job to be of greater importance as a motivational factor than Herzberg's achievement of growth variables. The British study, accordingly, both supports and provides an extension of the Herzberg theory.[18]

Finally, a study of job satisfaction among Saudi bureaucrats found money to be the major source of job dissatisfaction but group norms to be the main factor determining productivity. [19]

Placed in comparative and theoretical focus, then, the apparent contradiction between the emergence of low salaries as the primary source of job dissatisfaction among Egyptian bureaucrats and prestige as the preferred motivational value finds its explanation in the proposition that the stimuli to complain may differ substantially from the stimuli to produce. They involve different psychological processes that may or may not be related. The high incidence of supplemental jobs among Egyptian bureaucrats is also explained by established theories of motivation as well as by the grim reality of bureaucratic salary structures in Egypt. The stimulus for supplemental income is essentially the stimulus for survival. It is difficult to maintain a minimally acceptable lifestyle on government salaries. The fact that bureaucrats seek supplemental positions out of necessity does not contradict the dominant position of prestige as a motivational value once tolerable salary and related hygienic considerations have been achieved. Moreover, it is important to recall that the motivation scale presented in Table 3.7 assumes at least a minimally adequate salary level. The choice is not between prestige and a low salary, but between prestige and a moderate salary. As a general rule, human needs involving physical deprivation are more immediate and take preference over psychological needs for prestige, growth, and self-actualization. As such, they tend to block realization of needs for recognition and growth. Similarly, the mass migration of Egyptian bureaucrats to lucrative positions in the Gulf is not motivated by the promise of two or three salary increments. The stimulus for migration is the hope of attaining a radical transformation in lifestyles. Mass migration to the Gulf does not contradict the importance of prestige incentives in a bureaucratic setting. Moreover, our experience indicates that most migrants to the Gulf take leaves from their official positions and often return to their bureaucratic positions. A tour of duty in the Gulf tends to make a bureaucratic position affordable.

Based upon the above discussion, it is possible to offer the following observations concerning the utility of monetary incentives in the Egyptian bureaucracy.

1. The inordinately low salary structure of the Egyptian bureaucracy undermines productivity by forcing bureaucrats to divide their energies and talents between several positions. A substantial increase in government salaries would reduce the need for supplemental incomes and would make it easier for supervisors to demand higher levels of performance. Clearing the path to higher performance, however, does not guarantee that individuals will follow that path without further inducement.

2. Studies of motivation in the United States have long maintained that monetary incentives are difficult to implement in complex public bureaucracies. In particular, governments seldom possess sufficient resources to provide major incentives for more than a small portion of the bureaucracy. Given the reality of Egypt's financial position, it is highly unlikely that government monetary incentives can compete with the salaries of the private sector or the far larger rewards of the Gulf. Individuals essentially motivated by money are unlikely to remain in the bureaucracy, be it in Egypt or in the West.

3. Prestige and recognition incentives have been found to be effective in a variety of settings. The emergence of prestige as the dominant motivational value among our respondents suggests that prestige-based incentives may also be effective in Egypt. Indeed, the strength of prestige as a motivational value provides the opportunity for the Egyptian government to experiment with an incentive system that is both salient to its employees and feasible in the context of limited government resources.

4. Current salary structures in Egypt are so low that they

would, in all likelihood, reduce the effectiveness of prestige incentives. It is difficult to feed a family on prestige alone. Accordingly, prestige based incentives would probably be more effective if accompanied by a general increase in bureaucratic salaries. Alternatively, it might prove feasible to reinforce prestige-based incentives with a monetary component.

4

ℳ

Bureaucratic Flexibility and Development in Egypt

Bureaucratic flexibility is central to the developmental capacity of any bureaucracy. Flexibility enhances the ability of a bureaucracy to respond promptly and efficiently to the needs of the public. In so doing, bureaucratic flexibility strengthens rapport between the masses and the government and enhances public confidence in and cooperation with the bureaucratic apparatus. Bureaucratic flexibility also reduces waste by improving both the allocation of scarce resources and the coordination of bureaucratic efforts. And, bureaucratic flexibility facilitates bureaucratic innovation by making it possible for government officials to experiment with new and innovative approaches to the developmental needs of their society.

The Egyptian situation, as discussed at length in chapters 1 and 2, would clearly benefit from greater rapport between the masses and the government, from enhanced cooperation between the bureaucracy and the public, from less waste of very scarce resources, from better coordination of bureaucratic efforts, and from greater bureaucratic innovation in finding solutions for Egypt's myriad social and economic problems. Few criticisms of the Egyptian bureaucracy, however, have been as pervasive or as intense as criticism relating to its rigidity and inflexibility.[1]

A particularly vivid illustration of the rigidity of the Egyptian bureaucracy is to be found in an analysis of Cairo's utilities provided

An earlier version of this chapter appeared in *Public Administration and Development* 5, no. 4 (1985), pp. 323–37.

by the weekly magazine *Al Mussawar*.[2] In analyzing the reasons why a new pumping station was forced to operate at 50 percent of capacity due to exploding water mains, for example, *Al Mussawar* offered the following list of explanations, most of which focus directly upon problems of bureaucratic rigidity.

1. Difficulty in obtaining work permits.
2. Delays in clearances for digging under railroad, metro, and sewer lines.
3. Lack of skilled technicians and labor.
4. Shortages of wood and cement at the proper times.
5. Inadequate production of water pipe locally and severe difficulty in obtaining permits to import pipe.
6. The unwillingness of the water utility to coordinate with other utilities.
7. The absence of a clear map of the existing water network, a problem exacerbated by the existence of inaccurate maps.

The water utility, the *Al Mussawar* article goes on to note, is typical of all Cairo utilities. Each utility, according to the article, is a "world unto itself," jealously guarding its own preserve by denying information and cooperation to its sister utilities. The result of this situation is inordinate delays in the completion of all projects, disruption of services resulting from broken pipes and lines, wasted resources, and excessive cost overruns that the Egyptian government can ill afford. In regard to the latter, the article suggests that delays and confusion in coordinating the work of Cairo's utilities with the subway project costs the latter approximately $500,000 per week in fines and delays.

Problems of coordination and inflexibility, as Ayubi, Youssef, and others point out, are not unique to the utilities.[3] Rigidity is a malaise that afflicts the bureaucracy as a whole. It is a systemic problem. And, precisely because it is a systemic problem, the rigidity of the bureaucracy as an entity frustrates the efforts of the more energetic and innovative subunits by denying them the coordination and support they require to achieve their goals. Problems of rigidity must be attacked at the systemic as well as at the unit level.

There can be little doubt that a fair measure of Egypt's bureaucratic rigidity can be attributed to structural and environmental causes. The laws governing bureaucratic policy are often old, rigid, confused, and to some degree, contradictory.[4] The organizational structure of the bureaucracy, relatively simple under the monarchy, swelled to several times its original size during the socialist years or the Nasser regime. In the rush for development, new units were added to the old in response to the needs of the moment. It was a time of action that sought to circumvent bureaucratic delays by creating task-oriented units to compensate for the obstructionism of the main-line bureaucracy. Duplication of functions and confused lines of authority would be sorted out with time. Time, however, was always of the essence. Bureaucratic reforms, while often initiated, were overwhelmed by the greater concerns of war and peace. As things now stand, it is unlikely that the dramatic increases in productivity and development so ardently desired by President Mubarak can be achieved without a major rationalization of Egypt's bureaucratic apparatus.

Structural problems, unfortunately, are only one dimension of bureaucratic rigidity in Egypt. Rigidity also results from a variety of behavioral factors including the tendency of supervisors to concentrate as much authority as possible in their own hands and the corresponding tendency of subordinates to assume as little responsibility as possible. It is to the behavioral dimensions of bureaucratic rigidity in Egypt that the present chapter is devoted. Specifically, the present chapter examines three dimensions of behavioral rigidity within the Egyptian bureaucracy: (1) tendencies toward concentration of authority by supervisory officials, (2) the reluctance of subordinate officials to assume responsibility, and (3) the behavioral dimensions of communication within the bureaucracy.

Concentration of Authority

Egyptian officials are often criticized for attempting to concentrate as much authority as possible in their own hands. The authority that is delegated tends to be of limited quantity and duration. Little of any consequence occurs in the Egyptian administrative setting without the knowledge and direct consent of the supervisor.

If the centralization of authority by Egyptian officials is as severe as critiques in the Egyptian press suggest, it is clearly a major factor restricting the flexibility of the Egyptian bureaucracy. Among other things, the excessive concentration of authority creates administrative bottlenecks as supervisors compete to enlarge their respective domains. Excessive concern for authority and control preoccupies supervisors with matters of minor consequence, thereby restricting time available for tasks of major import. Supervisory officials in Egypt tend to be perpetually busy. Their time, however, is not always well spent.

Just as excessive concentration of authority overburdens senior officials, it also results in the underuse of the time and talents of subordinates. Tasks that could be readily executed by subordinates often sit on their desks awaiting instructions from above. Subordinates, in the meantime, content themselves with "busywork." Much of the behavior that is classified as bureaucratic apathy or laziness by casual observers is, in reality, merely idle time spent waiting for directions from on high. In the same manner, low levels of innovation in the Egyptian bureaucracy are at least partially explained by the limited scope for independent action enjoyed by most Egyptian employees.

Moreover, excessive concentration of authority is a major source of the red tape or routinization that has become the hallmark of Egyptian bureaucracy. As such, it is also one of the major sources of tension between the Egyptian bureaucracy and the public. It is truly difficult for the average Egyptian to develop supportive attitudes toward an apparatus that moves as ponderously as the Egyptian bureaucracy. Excessive concentration of authority also perpetuates the desire of the Egyptian public to go directly to the top of the administrative hierarchy, bypassing junior officials generally viewed as ineffective. "Going to the top," in turn, increases the demands placed upon supervisors and further reduces their ability to concentrate on issues of major import.

A number of our Egyptian colleagues felt that excessive concentration of authority had other undesirable influences upon the Egyptian bureaucracy as well. Some suggested that centralization increased the practice of *wasta* (influence) by focusing authority in the hands of a single exceptionally powerful individual. *Wasta,* if all else failed, could lead to a reordering of busy priorities. This is not to imply that all Egyptian officials are corrupt. This is clearly not the case. It is not to suggest that *wasta* would disappear with a greater decentralization of authority either. The centralization of authority, however, is clearly part of the problem.

Other colleagues suggested that the excessive concentration of authority reinforces tendencies toward dictatorial behavior within the bureaucracy and, in so doing, perpetuates the passiveness of junior officials, a passiveness already well established in Egyptian bureaucratic culture. The intimidation of employees, in turn, reduces tendencies toward risk taking and drives employees to seek security in the slavish adherence to routine. It also reinforces the tendency of subordinates to avoid responsibilities that might leave them vulnerable to the wrath of a tyrannical supervisor. Moreover, it was suggested that excessive concentration of authority fosters the development of patron–client networks. Such networks result in the evaluation of subordinates on the basis of loyalty to the supervisor rather than meritorious performance.

The concentration of authority, one might note, is not without its merits. The concentration of authority does enable an energetic and innovative supervisor to produce results that might otherwise be impossible given the overall lethargy of the Egyptian bureaucracy. Moreover, later analysis will indicate that the senior level of the Egyptian bureaucracy is its most energetic and most innovative component. By and large, hwoever, the advantages of greater flexibility would seem to far outweigh the advantages of excessive centralization. Also, the beneficial dimensions of concentrated authority may be of limited duration.

An Assessment of Centralization in the Egyptian Bureaucracy

Given the potential importance of the concentration of authority as a factor restricting the flexibility and developmental capacity of the Egyptian bureaucracy, one of the main objectives of the Al Ahram study was to provide an empirical assessment of the extent to which Egyptian officials did, indeed seek to concentrate as much authority as possible in their own hands. In line with popular wisdom and the experience of those who deal with the bureaucracy on a regular basis, we hypothesized that the concentration of authority would be a problem of major proportions.

The Al Ahram survey approached the problem of the concentration of authority from two perspectives. First, senior officials were requested to indicate the percentage of their peers "who felt it necessary to concentrate authority in their own hands." Second, the senior officials were presented with three questionnaire items designed to reflect their own tendencies toward the concentration of authority. Both the questionnaire items and the resulting response patterns are presented in Table 4.1.

The results in Table 4.1 support the popular assumption that bureaucratic authority is heavily centralized. Approximatley 65 percent of the respondents indicated that a majority of their colleagues found it necessary to concentrate authority under their personal control. Even more illustrative of centralizing tendencies were the three questionnaire items referring directly to the personal preferences of the senior respondents. Item 2 in Table 4.1, for example, indicates that, for one reason or another, some 85 percent of our senior respondents preferred to concentrate authority in their own hands. In the same manner, all but a handful of respondents also felt that training programs should stress technical skills rather than issues such as the delegation of authority.

Centralizing tendencies, then, are clearly manifest in the Egyptian bureaucracy. Moreover, as the results of question 3 in Table 4.1 indicate, they are present in spite of a frank admission by senior bureaucrats that their attempts to delgate authority have generally had a positive outcome. It could be argued, of course, that attempts to delegate authority have been beneficial largely because the authority in question was delegated with such care and reluctance.

Some Explanations of Centralizing Behavior

Attempts to explain why Egyptian officials seek to concentrate as much authority as possible in their own hands took two forms. First, the topic was discussed informally with a number of senior bureaucrats including a seminar of veteran senior officials who convened to discuss the results of the survey. Second, a block of questionnaire items requested our senior respondents to evaluate the relative importance of the most frequently encountered explanations for the concentration of authority.

Explanations of the concentration of authority by the participants in the seminar and by other Egyptian consultants stressed three themes. The first theme was historical in nature. Egypt, from earliest times, it was suggested, had been organized along hierarchical lines. No real precedents or models existed for the delegation of authority.

Table 4.1

Centralization of Decision Making (Senior Officials Only)
(n = 156)

1. In your experience, what percent of the administrators with whom you are acquainted find it necessary to centralize authority under their personal control?

	%
76–100%	26.6
51–75%	37.0
26–50%	20.1
Less than 25%	16.2
nonresponse = 1	100.0★

2. Given the situation as it currently exists in the Egyptian bureaucracy, do you feel that decision-making authority should be concentrated in the hands of senior officials or delegated to lower ranks?

a. Concentrated with senior officials	6.1
b. Delegated only as much as necessary	49.0
c. Delegated to the extent that delays and inconvenience do not result	30.6
d. Delegate as much as possible	14.3
nonresponse = 8	100.0

3. Have your personal attempts to delegate authority:

a. Caused major problems	3.3
b. Caused minor problems	20.9
c. Very helpful	75.8
nonresponse = 2	100.0

4. Do you believe training programs should stress:

a. Technical skills	92.7
b. Delegation of authority	7.3
nonresponse = 5	100.0

★Totals may vary from 100% owing to rounding error.

This theme is also elaborated in Ayubi's *Bureaucracy and Politics in Contemporary Egypt.*

The second theme stressed the patriarchal nature of Egyptian culture. The father rules the Egyptian family with absolute authority just as Egyptian leaders have traditionally ruled Egypt with absolute authority. Anwar Sadat, for example, referred to the Egyptian population as his children. Cultural patterns stressing paternal and political authoritarianism thus find a natural extension in bureaucratic behavior. Cultural explanations also stress the docility with which the average Egyptian employee accepts the dominance of the supervisor and, indeed, prefers to avoid assuming authority that would pose a challenge to the supervisor's dominance. Once attaining a supervisory position, however, employees demand the same deference from their subordinates. It is their right.

A third theme raised in our informal discussions of the causes of the concentration problem suggested that the desire of officials to concentrate authority was motivated by personal concerns of *wasta* and power. As the focal point of authority, the supervisor becomes the prime recipient of *wasta*. Moreover, power and respect in bureaucratic circles tend to be measured in terms of the range of affairs under an official's direct control. The more authority is delegated, according to this logic, the more *wasta* and respect devolve to subordinates, and the more supervisors are vulnerable to both the errors and the deliberate connivance of their subordinates. The concentration of authority, then, is viewed by some officials as a pragmatic necessity.

The second approach to explaining the desire of Egyptian officials to concentrate authority involved requesting senior officials to evaluate the relative importance of five major causes of centralization. It was impossible, of course, to include the question of *wasta* in this list. The relevant questionnaire items and response patterns for this phase of the analysis appear in Table 4.2. The results indicate that the major reason cited by senior officials for the concentration of authority was the technical inability of subordinates to execute the tasks delegated. Such explanations do have a base in empirical reality, yet we would note that the vast majority of the respondents surveyed did have at least high school educations. Indeed, 53 percent had attended college. Closely following low skill levels as an explanation of the concentration of authority was the reluctance of subordinates to

Table 4.2

Some Explanations of Centralization (Senior Bureaucrats Only)
(n = 156)

	Strongly Agree	Agree	Disagree	Strongly Disagree
1. Subordinates are reluctant to accept responsibility	30.9%	31.5%	30.2%	7.4%*
nonresponse = 5				
2. Subordinates lack skills to carry out the tasks delegated	23.6	53.4	18.9	4.1
nonresponse = 6				
3. Delegating authority causes confusion and delays	18.2	25.7	43.9	12.2
nonresponse = 6				
4. Subordinates misuse authority	25.0	43.9	24.3	6.8
nonresponse = 6				
5. Administrators who centralize authority are more respected (have more power) than those who do not	19.0	18.4	38.8	23.8
nonresponse = 7				

*Totals may vary from 100% owing to rounding error.

accept responsibility. The avoidance of responsibility was followed in close order by the fears of supervisors that their subordinates might very well misuse their authority. A full 68 percent of the senior officials expressed this fear.

Concentration of personal authority, then, is very evident in the Egyptian bureaucracy. Moreover, the sources of this problem are rooted both in the pragmatic realities of bureaucratic life as well as in the broader culture of Egyptian society.

The Avoidance of Responsibility

In contrast to the concentration of authority by supervisors, subordinate officials in Egypt are reputed to shun responsibility. The avoidance of responsibility by Egyptian officials takes a variety of guises, three of which are particularly prominent. First is the reputed tendency of officials to send all matters, large or small, to their supervisor for clearance. What the supervisor approves can cause little grief to the subordinate. The fact that such clearances take inordinate amounts of time and overload supervisors with minor details is of little concern to subordinate officials. A lack of time is not their problem. Second is the reputed tendency of subordinate officials to hide behind the rigidity and complexity of Egypt's bureaucratic codes. Demands that do not fit a clearly specified regulation tend to be either ignored or, more probably, set aside for further clarification. As such, rules and regulations are used as a sword against supervisors and the public alike. Finally, subordinates are reputed to avoid responsibility by a process best described as "foot dragging." Or, they may find themselves preoccupied with other priority tasks that would have to be delayed for the sake of the new request. Subordinates may plead inadequate skill to accomplish the task delegated. Or, technical and legal complications may arise that require clarification. The possibilities are endless.

If the avoidance of responsibility by subordinate officials is as severe as our consultants suggest, it must also be considered a major factor limiting the flexibility and, *ipso facto,* the developmental capacity of the Egyptian bureaucracy. The reluctance of subordinates to assume responsibility reinforces tendencies toward the excessive concentration of authority by supervisors. It overloads supervisory officials with petty details, robbing them of time and energies that could be devoted to more important matters. It forces clients "to go to the top" in search of solutions to their problems. In short, the reluctance of subordinates to assume responsibility reinforces and exacerbates all of the flexibility problems resulting from the reluctance of supervisory officials to delegate authority.

An Assessment of Responsibility Avoidance

The Al Ahram survey employed three diverse approaches to test the hypothesis that subordinate officials were prone to avoid responsibility. First, senior officials were requested to assess the magnitude of the responsibility avoidance problem. Second, middle- and lower-level officials were asked a battery of questions designed to assess the performance norms of their units. Several of the items in this scale were specifically concerned with problems of responsibility avoidance. Finally, middle- and lower-level officials were asked two questions relating to their willingness to execute orders that required a flexible interpretation of existing rules.

The Al Ahram survey contained two items requesting senior administrators to assess the problem of responsibility avoidance. The first, appearing as part of the battery of questions presented in Table 4.2, asked respondents to indicate the extent to which responsibility avoidance by subordinates contributed to excessive centralization by supervisors. As noted in Table 4.2, 62 percent of the respondents indicated that responsibility avoidance was an important contributing factor to the concentration of authority problem. A parallel question asked senior respondents to indicate the extent to which responsibilty avoidance contributed to low levels of innovation within the Egyptian bureaucracy. In this instance, 70 percent of the respondents indicated that responsibility avoidance was an important reason for the low innovation levels of the Egyptian bureaucracy. There can be little doubt then, that senior Egyptian bureaucrats perceived the avoidance of responsibility by their subordinates to be a major problem confronting the bureaucracy.

The group dynamics scale (Table 3.2) assesses group performance norms and thereby provides a view of the responsibility avoidance problem from the employee's perspective. The scores appearing in Table 3.2 reflect a weighting of Likert scale items to give "strongly agree" responses twice the weight of "agree" responses. Scores thus range from 0 to 100 with scores of 30 or less being in the critical problem range. It is interesting to note that subordinates give themselves relatively high marks in terms of their willingness to accept responsibility. From their perspective, a far more serious problem is the reluctance of supervisors to delegate authority. Even more revealing, however, are the extremely low scores for what might be termed the components of accepting responsibility: willingness to take risks, flexibility in executing decisions, and a willingness to accept conflict. In each of the three areas, scores were in the "critical" range. Taken collectively then, the results of the group dynamic scale suggest that Egyptian officials are willing to accept new responsibilities and new ideas as long as the new responsibilities do not involve conflict, risk, or flexibility.

To assess the problems of hiding behind rules and "foot dragging," the questionnaire contained two items designed to indicate how subordinates would cope with demands they disagreed with. The text and percentage distributions of the two items appear in Table 4.3. The responses to the first item indicate that subordinates were extraordinarily resistant to supervisory demands to bend existing rules for the sake of greater flexibility. Indeed, only 12 percent of the respondents indicated a willingness to make such adjustments without comment. One-half agreed to bend the rules, but only if the supervisor accepted responsibility for the act. The results of the second item indicate that 80 percent of the respondents would follow a solution they disagreed with, but only 3 percent would do so without argument. Particularly interesting in both items was the percentage of respondents who indicated that they would seek outside support against their supervisor. In the case of the supervisor demanding a bending of the rules, 17 percent of the respondents indicated that they would seek external support for their position. In the second case, involving a difference of opinion between the supervisor and the subordinate, 11 percent of the respondents indicated they would seek external support for their positions. Resistance to efforts of supervisors to impose their will upon their subordinates, then, is formidable. It does not augur well for the flexibility of the Egyptian bureaucracy.

The avoidance of responsibility is not a particularly difficult problem to understand, for it serves a variety of ends. In large part, the avoidance of responsibility by lower officials is the logical counterpart of the desire by supervisors to concentrate authority. Responsibility cannot reside in two places at the same time, and most but not all subordinates display little inclination to arouse the ire of their supervisors. Passivity is not an unwelcome virtue in many bureaucratic circles. Indeed, subordinates that are too anxious to assume additional responsibilities may be viewed with suspicion by their supervisors. As noted in the discussion of centralization, approximately 60 percent of the senior officials surveyed indicated that subordinates tended to misuse their authority. In effect, then, the concentration of authority by supervisory officials and the avoidance of responsibility by subordinates are part and parcel of the same process. One feeds upon the other. As such, it would probably be difficult to cure one without addressing the other.

Table 4.3

Responsibility Avoidance among Egyptian Bureaucrats
(Middle- and Lower-level Bureaucrats)
(n = 640)

1. If the efficiency of your unit is slowed by red tape and your supervisor asks you to bend the regulations for the sake of greater efficiency, what would you do?

   a. Seek the support of others in trying to follow the rules as they are written — 17.5

   b. Quietly follow the rules in spite of your supervisor's request — 20.6

   c. Bend the rules, but only under the condition that he accepts the responsibility for the changes — 48.6

   d. Accept your supervisor's request without comment — 12.0

   e. Other — .8

   100.0★

   nonresponse = 1

2. If you disagree with your supervisor on the best way to handle a problem, what would you do?

   a. Accept his solution without comment — 3.2

   b. Try to convince him of your point of view, but follow his solution — 80.9

   c. Quietly but firmly stick to your solution — 3.5

   d. Seek support for your position from other officials — 11.6

   e. Other — .8

   100.0

   nonresponse = 5

★Totals may vary from 100% owing to rounding error.

The penchant of subordinate officials to dodge responsibility has other causes as well. Responsibility means added work. Few Egyptian officials feel that their meager salaries justify added work. School teachers, to add a point of reference, receive the equivalent of $40 per month. One senior official expressed the sentiment as, "we pay them so little, how can I ask them to do more?"

Finally, in assessing the problem of responsibility avoidance, the senior officials surveyed placed great emphasis on the fact that many subordinate officials were poorly trained and lacked the experience to execute a wide range of responsibilities. In spite of the fact that many of Egyptian officials are university graduates, staffing procedures tend to be haphazard. The fit between skill and responsibility is poor, thereby reducing the utility of the technical expertise that is available.

Flexibility and Bureaucratic Communications

In addition to problems relating to the concentration of authority, the flexibility of a bureaucracy and its capacity to achieve its goals depend to a large extent upon its ability to process information in an effective manner. Without adequate information, officials find it difficult to perform their functions efficiently. Similarly, poor communications make the coordination of bureaucratic units marginal at best.

Communications within a bureaucracy are both an organizational and behavioral problem. The structural obstacles to communication and co-coordination within the Egyptian bureaucracy are analyzed extensively in Ayubi's *Bureaucracy and Politics in Contemporary Egypt* and are too complex to discuss at length at this point.

From a behavioral perspective, the Al Ahram questionnaire sought to examine the flow of communications and information both vertically between supervisors and subordinates and horizontally among subordinates. It was hypothesized that problems existed at both levels. In terms of vertical communications between supervisors and subordinates, the concern of the Al Ahram project was to examine levels of rigidity and flexibility in supervisor-subordinate relations. Excessively impersonal communication patterns would suggest rigidity and formalism and would aggravate the myriad problems of bureaucratic rigidity reviewed earlier. More personalized communication patterns, by contrast, would suggest a warmer working relationship between supervisors and subordinates, a relationship that would allow supervisors to manage their subordinates by informal techniques of persuasion and positive reinforcement rather than by merely relying upon the rigid application of authority.

The results of the vertical communication items are striking. The data presented in Table 4.4 indicate that approximately one-half

Table 4.4

Vertical Communications
(n = 796)

1. How often do you discuss official matters with your immediate supervisor?

		%
a.	Rarely	6.8
b.	Occasionally	46.0
c.	Frequently	27.0
d.	Daily	20.3
		100.0*

nonresponse = 1

2. How often do you discuss informal or personal matters with your immediate supervisors?

		%
a.	Never	74.1
b.	Occasionally	23.8
c.	Frequently	1.4
d.	Daily	.8
		100.0

nonresponse = 1

*Totals may vary from 100% owing to rounding error.

of the respondents consulted with their supervisors on work-related matters on a frequent if not daily basis. Less than 3 percent of the respondents, by contrast, discussed informal or personal matters with their supervisors on more than an occasional basis. Seventy-five percent of the respondents never discussed informal or personal affairs with their immediate supervisor. An elaboration of this theme is to be found in the analysis of reference group patterns, the percentage distributions for which are provided in Table 4.5. In this particular instance, one finds less than 5 percent of the respondents listing their

Table 4.5

Horizontal Communications
(n = 796)

Sometimes one needs to speak with another person about one's personal affairs and problems. To you, who is this other?

	Weighted Score	First Choice	Second Choice
1. Family members	67	61.6	9.8
2. Friends	30	18.4	22.4
3. Colleagues in job	12	5.0	15.4
4. Colleagues in the club	1	0.4	1.6
5. Relatives (distant)	11	1.6	19.0
6. Boss	3	0.8	4.4
7. Consultants	14	4.8	17.8
8. None	1	6.8	9.5
		100%★	100%

nonresponse = 25

If you face a personal problem with a government agency and need someone to help you, to whom do you go?

1. Family members	37	30.9	12.1
2. Job colleagues	51	35.5	30.7
3. Club colleagues	3	1.3	.1
4. Relatives (distant)	0	2.2	13.3
5. My supervisor at work	43	26.4	33.3
6. Political leaders	5	2.5	4.1
7. Religious leaders	3	1.3	3.4
		100%	100%

nonresponse = 19

★Totals may vary from 100% owing to rounding error.

supervisors as an individual with whom they were likely to discuss their personal affairs. It is interesting to note, however, that more than 50 percent of the respondents listed their supervisor as the individual with whom they would consult if they had a problem with a government agency.

Taken collectively, the responses to the vertical communication items reinforce the conclusions of the earlier discussion of the concentration of authority. First, the lack of informal communications between subordinates and supervisors concerning matters of a personal or an informal nature would clearly limit opportunities for the use of informal motivational and supervisory mechanisms stressed by Western theories of management.[5] They would also appear to reinforce the image of the "supervisor as tyrant" portrayed in the editorial quoted in chapter 2. Second, the high incidence of dependence upon supervisors for advice concerning problems with a government agency suggests the clear presence of patron-client relationships as well as an extremely high dependence on the use of *wasta* or influence. It also suggests that the passivity of subordinates is reinforced by their dependency upon patron-client relationships in assisting with government-related problems. Such problems, one might note, are not infrequent.

Efforts to examine horizontal communications among officials of the same level were also designed to ascertain whether work relations were of a formal or of a personal nature. Within the limits of the data presented in Table 4.5, it might be suggested that horizontal relations are also formal. While employees consult each other frequently on job-related items and assist one another in dealing with government agencies, less than 20 percent of the respondents listed their colleagues as individuals to whom they would turn with a personal problem. At the very least, the data suggest that family bonds continue to be the primary bonds of Egyptian society, bonds of far greater strength than the interpersonal ties created by work relationships. Such inferences, however, are impaired by the absence of comparative norms. The data are offered for informational purposes and to provide base-line data for further research.

Conclusion

The Egyptian bureaucracy has been criticized by the press, by scholars and by our consultants for being excessively rigid. This rigidity was said to stem from (1) the desire of supervisors to concentrate authority in their own hands, (2) the reluctance of subordinates to assume responsibility, and (3) the formal pattern of communications that exists within the bureaucracy. The Al Ahram survey examined bureaucratic behavior in each of the above problem areas. In each case the survey results sustained the accusations: supervisors do tend to concentrate as much authority as possible in their own hands, subordinates do tend to shun responsibilty, and informal communications patterns within the bureaucracy are rigid. This is particularly the case in regard to comunications between supervisors and subordinates.

The results of the survey do not reflect well upon the developmental capacity of the Egyptian bureaucracy. In particular, the Egyptian bureaucracy may find it difficult to perform the tremendous developmental responsibilities being placed upon its shoulders without both a greater willingness by supervisors to delegate authority and a corresponding willingness by subordinates to accept responsibility. A marked increase in informal communication between subordinates and supervisors would also appear to be an important step in this direction.

5

✍

Innovation and Bureaucracy in Egypt

Up to this point we have painted a picture of a bureaucratic apparatus that is both lethargic and rigid. Things get done, but they get done slowly. Faced with a growing array of social and political pressures, the bureaucracy somehow finds a way to muddle through.

The Egyptian bureaucracy, however, must do more than muddle through. Egypt's social and economic problems are staggering. Moreover, as the bureaucracy struggles to maintain vital services at minimally adequate levels, it increasingly abdicates its role as Egypt's primary agent of economic and social development. A country mired in debt and faced with a million new souls each year can ill afford to neglect the developmental needs of the future.

If Egypt is to keep pace with the basic needs of its burgeoning population, and if it is to provide a viable social and economic foundation for future generations, it is essential that the bureaucracy provide new and innovative solutions to Egypt's mounting social and economic problems. The old ways simply are not working.

Viewed in this light, three fundamental questions arise concerning the innovative capacity of the Egyptian bureaucracy. First, is the bureaucracy predisposed to seek new and innovative solutions to Egypt's social and economic problems? Second, do decision-making procedures within the bureaucracy facilitate innovation and change? Third, how can the bureaucracy's innovative capacity be increased?

In an effort to provide answers to these and related questions, the present chapter will (1) assess levels of innovation within the Egyptian bureaucracy, (2) explain some of the reasons for low innovation within the bureaucracy, and (3) identify the most innovative elements within the bureaucracy. In pursuing these objectives it should also be possible to suggest ways in which the innovative capacity of the bureaucracy can be strengthened.

Assessing Bureaucratic Innovation in the Egyptian Setting

In line with the discussion of bureaucratic culture (chapter 2), it was hypothesized that the level of innovation within the Egyptian bureaucracy would be low indeed. Unfortunately, it is not possible to hypothesize that the level of innovation is below established developmental norms, for such comparative norms do not exist.[1] The purpose of assessing levels of innovation within the Egyptian bureaucracy, it should be noted, is not merely to belabor the obvious. While it is generally assumed that the Egyptian bureaucracy is noninnovative, efforts to improve this situation require an empirical assessment of the problem. Just how bad is the situation? Perhaps the bureaucracy is far more innovative than people believe. Moreover, how does one identify the more innovative elements within the bureaucracy without a prior assessment of innovation levels within the bureaucracy as a whole?

However relevant innovation may be to the process of economic and social development, the concept of innovation, itself, remains vague and poorly defined.[2] Operational definitions vary markedly from field to field and from study to study. Studies of bureaucratic innovation, in particular, have been few and far between. In spite of some definitional vagueness, however, the core of the concept within the social sciences invariably focuses on the creation and implementation of new solutions to existing problems.

Because of the inherent vagueness of existing conceptualizations of innovation, the Al Ahram study approached the assessment of innovation within the Egyptian bureaucracy from four diverse perspectives. First, senior officials were requested to estimate the percentage of their subordinates "who attempted to innovate or try new ideas: Second, two items in the group dynamics scale (Table 3.2) were designed to provide a peer evaluation of the innovativeness of middle- and lower-level bureaucrats. Third, the respondents were presented with a series of questionnaire items designed to measure their predisposition to challenge those social practices and traditions that pose a obstacle to economic and social development. A willingness to

Table 5.1

Assessments of Bureaucratic Innovation
(n = 156; nonresponse = 4)

What is the percentage of your subordinates who attempt to innovate or try new ideas?

0–10%	61.2
11–25	19.7
26–50	13.2
51–100	5.9
	100%

n = 156

nonresponse = 4

challenge social traditions and practices was considered to be an important dimension of bureaucratic innovation in Egypt, for individuals receptive to social change are far more likely to suggest and support new ideas and programs than individuals wedded to the past. Fourth, respondents were presented with a series of questionnaire items designed to measure innovativeness and creativity in their everyday decision-making strategies.

The senior bureaucrats' assessments of the innovativeness of their subordinates are provided in Table 5.1. As might be expected, they supported the popular wisdom that innovation is not the strong suit of the Egyptian bureaucracy. Indeed, approximately 60 percent of the senior bureaucrats surveyed indicated that less than 10 percent of their subordinates were willing to innovate or try new ideas. An additional 20 percent of the respondents indicated that less than 25 percent of their subordinates were inclined to try new ideas. Such results hardly speak well for the innovative capacity of the Egyptian bureaucracy or for its ability to design and implement creative solutions to Egypt's massive social and economic problems.

The results of the innovation-related items in the group dynamics scale (Table 3.2) paint a similar picture. Only 9.3 percent of the

Table 5.2

Predispositions toward Social Innovation
(n = 796)

1. It is best to cancel or change programs that could cause social conflict.

    agree   89.8%

    disagree   10.2%   (nr = 1)

2. Social change should not be instituted at the expense of traditional values.

    agree   70.5
    disagree   29.5   (nr = 1)

3. Economic development should be pursued even if it means hardship for the majority of the people.

    agree   50.4
    disagree   49.6   (nr = 2)

4. We have tried too hard to copy the developmental programs of the West without worrying about our own heritage.

    agree   62.5
    disagree   37.5   (nr = 4)

5. Pursuing development too rapidly might be worse than developing too slowly.

    agree   74.1
    disagree   25.9   (nr = 2)

respondents, for example, strongly agreed that their peers were open to new ideas. In much the same manner, less than 8 percent of the respondents strongly agreed that their peers were willing to take risks. Indeed, the innovation-related items ranked very near to the bottom of the group dynamics scale.

Predispositions to challenge existing social values, in turn, were measured by a battery of five items, the text and percentage distributions for which appear in Table 5.2. The five items in Table 5.2 reflect a variety of considerations that the panel designing the questionnaire felt might deter Egyptian bureaucrats from taking an assertive and innovative posture in their decision making. The first item in Table

5.2, for example, assesses the bureaucrats' concern for social harmony, an issue of extreme sensitivity in government circles. Just how willing are Egypt's bureaucrats to venture into areas that might directly or inadvertently result in heightened social tensions? The answer was striking in its frankness, with some 90 percent of the respondents indicating that programs likely to cause or intensify social conflict should be canceled. The magnitude of this response can only be interpreted as an obstacle to bureaucratic innovation, for it is difficult to imagine viable solutions to Egypt's myriad economic and social problems that did not generate tensions among the Egyptian population. Rare indeed, it appears, is the bureaucrat willing to risk the ire of political officials by venturing into troubled waters.

In much the same manner, responses to item 5 in Table 5.2 indicate that a preponderance of Egyptian bureaucrats are very hesitant about plunging full speed into developmental programs when the outcome and duration are less than clear. In this regard it should be recalled that the Egyptian bureaucracy endured an intensive drive toward socialist-oriented modernization during the Nasser era only to be confronted with a decade of capitalism under Sadat. Signals from the Mubarak regime remain mixed.

Items 2 and 4, in turn, assessed the attachment of the respondents to traditional values, values generally viewed as being antithetical to the modernization process.[3] Again, a preponderance of the respondents felt that modernization programs should not alter traditional values, a mind set fully in line with Egypt's resurgent Islamic values. Individuals predisposed against change can hardly be expected to innovate on its behalf.

Finally, item 3 of Table 5.2 assessed the willingness of our respondents to impose hardships on the majority of the population for the sake of economic development. Respondents were evenly divided on this issue. On one hand, this result reflects a realization by many Egyptian bureaucrats that economic development is virtually impossible without the imposition of austerity measures and other programs that impose hardships on the masses. On the other hand, the same result also indicates that one-half of the respondents were very reluctant to see such measures instituted.

The five items appearing in Table 5.2 are not unidimensional. Accordingly, they were not scaled to provide an overall indicator of predispositions toward social innovation. Turning from predispositions toward innovation to assessments of innovative behavior in

Table 5.3

Innovation in Decision Making
(n = 796)

	Strongly Agree	Agree	Disagree	Strongly Disagree
1. Decision should stress harmony in the work group. nr = 10	65.4%	33.3%	1.3%	0%
2. It is probably best to consult with one's supervisor before making even small decisions. nr = 8	31.3	58.3	9.5	.9
3. One should follow the rules in order to get things done effectively. nr = 8	36.7	56.4	6.1	.8
4. In making new decisions, it is probably best to see what was done in the past. nr = 8	42.8	53.4	2.8	1.0
5. It is better to delay decisions than to risk making a mistake. nr = 8	27.2	47.3	20.0	5.5

Decision-Making Scale

Low-innovative	86.3
Moderate	13.5
High	.3

*Totals may very from 100% owing to rounding error.

routine decision-making situations, the respondents were asked a battery of five items relating to their everyday decision-making practices, the text and percentage distributions for which appear in Table 5.3. While no single item in the table would, of itself, condemn a respondent to the ranks of the noninnovative, respondents who answered most questions in the affirmative must be considered excessively rigid and noninnovative in their decision-making behavior. The five items in Table 5.3 were unidimensional and were scaled to form a "decision-making innovation scale." The innovation decision-making scale was a simple additive scale.

Responses to the five items that constitute the decision-making innovation scale reflect exceptionally low levels of innovation in the decision-making behavior of Egyptian officials. Indeed, only in item 5 did more than 11 percent of the respondents accept the innovative option. In terms of the decision-making scale score, 86 percent of the respondents fell in the low innovation category, with 13 percent achieving a moderate score. Only 1 percent of the respondents could be considered as high innovators on the basis of their routine decision-making practices. This suggests, of course, that the probability of innovation occuring as a result of the ongoing process of routine decision making is minimal. It also suggests that the capacity of officials to find innovative and flexible solutions to the daily problems of the Egyptian public is also low.

Explanations of Low Bureaucratic Innovation in the Middle East

The first step in improving levels of innovation among Egyptian civil servants is to understand the causes of their reluctance to innovate. In attempting this endeavor, we shall examine two types of explanations: scholarly explanations and practitioner explanations. By scholarly explanations we refer to the explanations provided by scholars who have attempted to fathom the problems of the bureaucracy from the outside. These explanations tend to be heavily social-psychological in nature and were reviewed at some length in chapter 2. Practitioner explanations, by contrast, focus on the practical experience of the senior officials surveyed. The former benefit from the body of social, developmental, and administrative theory that has been generated over the past several decades and that draws upon a universal base of experience. The latter draws upon the experience of individuals intimately familiar with the daily workings of their respective bureaucracies. There is no way to indicate which of the two points of view is the most valid. Quite clearly, the more they converge, the closer to the heart of the problem one is likely to be.

For analytical purposes, the explanations of low bureaucratic innovativeness will be divided into five categories: (1) systemic explanations, (2) cultural/personal explanations, (3) insecurity-related explanations, (4) group dynamic explanations, and (5) supervisor dynamic explanations.

Structural problems constitute the most visible and, consequently, the most analyzed dimension of the bureaucratic process in Egypt.[4] Foremost among the structural influences upon innovation is the question of salaries. Government salaries in Egypt no longer provide government employees with an adequate standard of living. Even more problematic is the growing gap in wages between the public and private sectors of the Egyptian economy. Not only are the wages of Egyptian civil servants low in absolute terms, but they are also low in relative terms. While Egyptian civil servants struggle to make ends meet, their counterparts in the newly revitalized private sector are living in comparative splendor. Salaries and related incentives such as promotions and bonuses, quite clearly, are central to the question of innovation. Simply stated, poorly paid employees have little incentive to try new ideas or to take unnecessary risks.

A second set of structural problems related to low levels of bureaucratic innovation in Egypt finds its origins in the welfare orientation of the Egyptian bureaucracy. To fully understand this situation, it must be recalled that Egypt uses bureaucratic staffing as a means of providing mass employment, the graduates policy being a case in point. Welfare rather than efficiency is the hallmark of bureaucratic recruitment in Egypt.

Welfare-oriented staffing policies influence bureaucratic innovation in three ways. First, welfare-based recruitment draws large numbers of poorly skilled individuals into the bureaucracy. Having low skill levels to begin with, they are poorly qualified to perform a wide range of tasks. Moreover, their low skill levels tend to make them insecure and reluctant to attempt tasks that will amplify their inadequacies and perhaps render them vulnerable to dismissal or disciplinary action. Regardless of predispositions toward innovation, poorly skilled individuals are not well positioned to engage in innovative behavior. Second, welfare-based recruitment leads to overstaffing and to the misallocation of those skills that are available. Misplaced skills are of little more utility than no skills at all. Third, welfare-based recruitment creates an environment of noncompetitive complacency. Government positions tend to be looked upon as a fiefdom, as something the recipient is entitled to by divine right. Competition breeds innovation; conformity stifles it. In this regard, one might recall the expectations of the respondents upon entering the bureaucracy. When asked what their friends and relatives felt to be the major advantages of government service, the list was headed by "permanent," 25 percent; "firm income," 25 percent; and "low hours," 17 percent, hardly values to be associated with innovation or risk taking (Table 2.1).

Salary levels and welfare-oriented recruitment are but two of the most obvious structural impediments to bureaucratic innovation in Egypt. Many Egyptian bureaucrats lack the authority to execute all but the most routine tasks, a situation exacerbated by the tendency of supervisory officials to concentrate as much authority as possible in their own hands. The situation is not eased by the morass of bureaucratic regulations and overlapping authority patterns that characterize the Egyptian bureaucracy either. Many Egyptian officials are sincerely confused about their responsibilities; others use ambiguous rules as a pretext for avoiding work or dodging responsibility. Either way, innovation suffers. Also, it should be noted that bureaucratic regulations in Egypt focus on sins of commission rather than sins of omission. It is far more dangerous to stick one's neck out than it is to do nothing.

Given the clear link between structural problems and low bureaucratic innovation, one might well be tempted to explain the low innovation levels of Egyptian bureaucrats solely on structural grounds. Such a conclusion, if valid, would mean that innovation could be substantially increased simply by means of structural reform. Indeed, salary increases, of themselves, might alleviate a lion's share of the problem.

Such optimism, unfortunately, appears to be premature. While there can be little doubt that structural problems do have a debilitating impact on innovation, there is little evidence to suggest that increased salaries or other structural reforms will, of themselves, increase innovation or motivation. Structural improvements may make it easier for workers to perform at a comfortable level, but such improvements are unlikely to push them beyond that level. This point has long been associated with the work of Frederick Herzberg and was discussed at length in chapter 3.[5] Herzberg's theory, if correct, would deal a severe blow to the hopes of those who feel that improving bureaucratic innovation in Egypt is merely a matter of improving salary structures and alleviating the various structural problems surveyed above.

In summarizing the influence of structural variables upon bureaucratic innovation in Egypt, it would seem logical to conclude that structural circumstances must be substantially improved in order to eliminate their negative impact on innovation. One must also conclude, however, that structural improvements are not sufficient of themselves to solve the problem of low innovation. One must probe deeper into the sources of bureaucratic behavior.

The cultural impediments to innovation find their origins in the attitudes and predispositions that government officials bring to their work. In this regard, the sociological and psychological literature is replete with explanations of why Egyptian officials should be less than innovative in solving the problems of their region. Topping the list of cultural explanations is the sense of fatalism that tends to pervade Egyptian society. If the affairs of man are regulated by God, the need for human innovation is minimal.[6] Related theories suggest that Egyptian society places a special emphasis on social conformity.[7] Early socialization patterns reward conformity, not creativity or innovation.

Yet a third set of social theories stress the poorly developed sense of work ethic or achievement motivation in Egypt and many other Middle Eastern societies.[8] According to this view, self-esteem in Middle Eastern societies is not necessarily tied to levels of material achievement. Egyptians, accordingly, are less likely than their Western counterparts to be driven by an internalized need for achievement. As innovation is one path to greater achievement, Egyptians are less likely to innovate than their Western counterparts. Finally, it might also be suggested that Egyptian society places greater emphasis on traditional values than do many Western societies. The past is to be valued. It is not to be discarded lightly. Change is not perceived as an unmitigated good. Social continuity rivals the desire for modernity and change.

It would be difficult to suggest that each of the above forces and their variants were equally applicable across the full spectrum of Egyptian culture. Nevertheless, sufficient literature on the topic exists to suggest that these themes, collectively, do provide a cultural bias against bureaucratic innovation. This is an important point, for cultural obstacles to bureaucratic innovation may be far more difficult to alter than structural obstacles to innovation. Indeed, cultural biases against innovation could well undermine structural reforms designed to increase innovation.

If cultural influences predispose the Egyptian bureaucrat to be noninnovative, those predispositions are clearly reinforced by the group dynamics in the work environment. Innovative individuals— and there are innovative individuals in the Egyptian bureaucracy— find their suggestions for change squelched by resentful peers jealous of the attention that accrues to the innovator or fearful that their daily routine might be jeopardized. Innovation in a hostile group environment is an uphill battle. It is a battle that must be fought by more than a handful of individuals, and it is a battle that must be reinforced by supervisors at all levels. Innovation levels in the Egyptian bureaucracy are also depressed by what Berger termed "the security consciousness of Middle Eastern bureaucracies."[9] A bureaucratic position in Egypt tends to be a sinecure: a base that provides its occupant with a stable salary, access to government circles, at least menial respect, and a very tolerable workload. Few Egyptian bureaucrats, according to Ayubi, are willing to jeopardize such a pleasing state of affairs by rocking the boat.[10] To quote an Egyptian proverb, "The more you work, the more errors you make." The same principle applies to innovation. In this regard, one might also recall the earlier observation that the insecurity of many Middle Eastern bureaucrats is heightened by inadequate skill levels.

Finally, noninnovative tendencies in the Egyptian bureaucracy are reinforced by the process of supervisor dynamics. Supervisors in Egypt, as observed in chapter 4, tend to concentrate as much authority as possible in their own hands. Little authority is delegated. Subordinates receive little positive reinforcement for work well done. Innovation and risk taking are not reinforced. Indeed, it would appear that many supervisory personnel in Egypt prefer subordinates who keep a low profile and who do not rock the boat. Subservience often brings greater rewards than hard work.

Explanations of Bureaucratic Apathy by Senior Officials

The manner in which senior officials view the problem of bureaucratic innovation is critically important for three basic reasons.

First and perhaps foremost, senior officials are those individuals directly responsible for initiating programs designed to increase bureaucratic innovation. Supervisors are far more likely to attack the problems they believe to cause low innovation than they are to implement programs of a theoretical nature suggested by outsiders. Second, senior officials are those individuals closest to the problem. Their opinions on the subject must be respected. Indeed, their perceptions may well be closer to the mark than the views of outside experts. Third, explanations of low innovation cited by both external experts and supervisory personnel are likely to be more accurate than the explanations cited by either the theorist or the practitioner alone.

Assessing the manner in which senior officials view the problem of low innovation was approached by asking senior bureaucrats to evaluate the importance of each of the theoretical explanations of low innovation discussed above. The results of these items are presented in Table 5.4. Table 5.4 contains two types of data: the percentage of respondents who felt that the explanation in question was "very important" and the percentage of respondents who felt the explanation in question was either "very important" or "important." The latter column is labeled "relevant."

The first and most important conclusion to be reached from the data presented in Table 5.4 is that all of the explanations suggested by the theoretical literature were considered relevant by a large number of senior officials. This finding, of itself, indicates a high level of congruity between the theoretical literature and the evaluations of the senior officials. It also suggests that senior officials are cognizant of the broader cultural and personality dimensions of the innovation problem, and that efforts to overcome the problem of low innovation may be complex, indeed. This being the case, it is unlikely that the problem of low bureaucratic innovation will be solved merely by structural adjustments or other "quick fixes." Considerations of culture, group dynamics, and supervisor dynamics must all be incorporated into programs designed to increase bureaucratic innovation.

Having noted a general awareness of the complexity of the innovation problem, it must also be noted that senior Egyptian officials attributed a lion's share of the problem to the low qualifications of their subordinates and the lack of adequate incentives. In the view of more than 90 percent of the senior officials, their subordinates were simply unqualified to innovate.

Though not rivaling skill levels in terms of importance, it was

Table 5.4

Explanations of Low Bureaucratic Innovation
(n = 156)

Systemic	VI*	R*
low skills	63.6%	96.1%
low incentives	70.8	94.2
Culture		
low concern for job	29.4	78.4
cultural bias	12.2	43.2
Risk/Security		
avoid responsibility	21.8	73.5
fear mistakes	26.4	79.1
Group Dynamics		
upset colleagues	8.5	43.8
no one else works	29.1	66.2
Supervisor Dynamics		
fear supervisor	28.4	58.1
lack authority	36.2	79.2

*VI Percent "Very Important"
*R Percent "Relevant" (very important or important)

interesting to note the prominence of subordinate insecurity as an obstacle to greater innovation. More than 70 percent of the Egyptian officials, for example, indicated that their subordinates were afraid of making mistakes that would leave them vulnerable to disciplinary action. This fear is also manifest in parallel results indicating that subordinate officials were reluctant to assume added responsibilities. Innovation, by the very nature of the beast, requires risk taking and the assumption of responsibility.

The climate of insecurity that pervades the Egyptian bureaucracy must ultimately find at least part of its cause in the climate of relations between supervisors and subordinates. As discussed at length in chapter 4, senior officials in Egypt do manifest a strong desire to concentrate as much authority as possible in their own hands. They are not prone to delegate authority, and they do worry about the misuse of authority by their subordinates. It should not be surprising then, that a clear majority of Egyptian officials did indicate that innovative tendencies were depressed by "fear of upsetting the supervisor." They also indicated that their employees lacked authority to innovate, a matter that could be easily remedied by the senior officials if they so desired. Both results suggest that the climate of supervisor-subordinate relations does little to promote innovation.

Cultural and psychological explanations were also perceived as relevant to the innovation problem. The major emphasis, however, was placed upon the "general disinterest of subordinates in their work" rather than upon a cultural bias against innovation. The same theme is reflected in the results of the group dynamics items, items which reflect a severe morale problem among Egyptian bureaucrats.

Indentifying the Innovators

While the Egyptian bureaucracy as a whole displayed little inclination toward innovation, it is probable that some elements within the bureaucracy are far more innovative than others. This is an important consideration, for efforts to increase the openness to innovation of any bureaucracy would logically seek to strengthen, extend, and emulate its most innovative elements. This topic is examined at length in chapter 7. Suffice it for the moment to say that the Egyptian buraucracy, as a whole, is predisposed against social innovation. In reference to the discussion of bureaucratic culture contained in chapter 2, it would seem that avoidance of social conflict and conservatism toward sweeping developmental programs are part and parcel of Egyptian bureaucratic culture. The bureaucracy is clearly predisposed to move slowly and with great care.

Decision-making innovation (Table 5.3) differs markedly from social innovation. The latter focuses on broad social values that ence a willingness to pursue and support the implementation of innovative developmental programs. The former, by contrast focuses on specific decision-making strategies. While predispositions toward both decision-making innovation and social innovation influence the capacity of the Egyptian bureaucracy to play an innovative role in the developmental process, they are essentially different phenomena. As one might expect from this difference of focus, the correlates of decision-making innovation were different from the correlates of predispositions toward social innovation. Because this is more of an individualized rather than a cultural phenomenon, tendencies toward decision-making innovation varied markedly on the basis of job level, age, and education. As will be elaborated in chapter 7, decision-making innovation was the strongest (although not strong) at the senior level of the bureaucracy. It is a rare commodity, indeed, among junior officials. Decision-making innovation also increased with age and education. The low levels of decision-making innovation at the lower levels of the bureaucracy are particularly unfortunate, for many opportunities for day-to-day innovation and for providing flexible solutions to client problems occur at the lower rather than the upper reaches of the bureaucratic structure. They also suggest that lower-level officials may be less than willing to implement innovative suggestions from their superiors unless they clearly conform to established procedures, a process discussed at some length in chapter 4. It might be recalled, for instance, that one of the questionnaire items presented in Table 4.3 asked middle- and lower-level officials how they would respond if their supervisor asked them to bend the rules for the sake of greater efficiency. The results, presented in Table 4.3, indicate that only 12 percent of the bureaucrats surveyed would comply with their supervisors' requests without objection.

Conclusion: Suggestions for Increasing the Innovative Capacity of the Egyptian Bureaucracy

The present chapter examined two dimensions of bureaucratic innovation: predispositions to make innovative decisions that had a major impact upon society and its values and creativity and flexibility in day-to-day decision making.

In regard to predispositions toward social innovation, the data indicated a pervasive reluctance at all levels of the bureaucracy to embark upon programs that would either increase social tensions or adversely affect traditional values. The general tenor of the bureaucracy was clearly one of caution, hardly a characteristic to be associated with the innovative pursual of far-reaching social and economic development programs. Inasmuch as the reluctance to pursue conflicting programs appeared to be deeply rooted within the Egyptian bureaucratic culture and varied little on the basis of education, job level, or training, it is difficult to suggest modes of improvement. The change of institutional values is a slow process.

The analysis of decision-making innovation also reflected low levels of innovation. Indeed, less that 1 percent of the respondents could be considered active innovators. The analysis of the most innovative elements within the bureaucracy and their attributes will be examined at length in chapter 7.

6

Bureaucracy and the Public

Most bureaucratic activity, directly or indirectly, involves interaction with the public. This is particularly the case in regard to the Egyptian bureaucracy, for it is the Egyptian bureaucracy that must modernize, mobilize, and otherwise integrate the Egyptian masses into the developmental programs of the state. It is inevitable, accordingly, that the developmental capacity of the Egyptian bureaucracy will be shaped by the quality of trust, cooperation, and mutual respect that exists between the bureaucracy and its clients.

Unfortunately, mutual trust, respect, and cooperation between the Egyptian bureaucracy and its clients appear to be in short supply. Indeed, President Mubarak's 1985 address to the Egyptian Parliament urged Egyptians to have faith in their bureaucracy. Many Egyptians, judging by the intensity of President Mubarak's comments, seriously doubt the ability of the bureaucracy to solve Egypt's economic problems.[1]

Egypt's political leaders, as President Mubarak's comments indicate, are keenly aware of the need to improve the quality of rapport and cooperation between the bureaucracy and the masses. Indeed, Dr. Ali Lutfi, former chairman of the Department of Economics at Ein Shams University and recently the Egyptian Prime Minister, listed improved cooperation between the bureaucracy and the masses as the first of ten preconditions essential for Egypt's economic development. Toward this end he urged that the following measures be initiated:

An earlier version of this chapter appeared in the *International Review of Administrative Sciences* 52, no. 3 (September 1986), pp. 325–38.

1. Providing the masses with frank information on the economic problems confronting the state and convincing them that the problems are capable of solution.
2. Discussing the required solutions with the masses in a simple and understandable manner.
3. Enlisting mass participation in finding solutions to the country's major economic problems, such as price supports and population growth.
4. Selecting officials (leaders) able to provide a positive example for the masses, leaders that will exemplify "clean hands, moderate tongue, decency, honesty, reliability, and frankness."
5. Selecting officials (leaders) who will provide true and scientific information concerning solutions to the nation's problems.
6. Distributing the burden of development justly and fairly among the masses.
7. Eliminating all "exceptions" to rules and policies in order that all Egyptians may feel that everyone has equal rights and equal opportunities.
8. Creating confidence among the citizens by making all citizens aware of their rights and obligations, so that Egypt can put an end to outdated customs which block the road to development.[2]

Dr. Lutfi's comments were but the latest in a long series of pleas for increased "public awareness" on the part of the bureaucracy. During the era of Sadat's administrative revolution, for example, an *Al Ahram* editorial called for an abolition of "All those regulations and laws governing economic activities (which) assume that every single Egyptian is a thief, every citizen is oblique and every human being is fraudulent."[3]

The lack of rapport between the bureaucracy and the Egyptian public has two basic components: a mass component and a bureaucratic component. The masses, as discussed in chapter 2, tend to view the bureaucracy with a skepticism born of decades of bureaucratic arrogance, self-service, and obstructionism. The bureaucracy, for its part, is wont to view the masses as critical, demanding, and obsessed with the pursuit of *wasta* and special favors. Each is content to blame the other for Egypt's burgeoning economic and social problems.

The improvement in rapport and cooperation between the bureaucracy and the Egyptian public demanded by President Mubarak clearly necessitates changes in the behavior of both parties to the conflict. From a realistic point of view, however, it is doubtful that mass attitudes toward either the bureaucracy or the government will change markedly without clear if not dramatic improvements in bureaucratic performance. The masses are passive and without a direct focus. It is the bureaucracy that has the capacity to act.

As a first step in addressing the conflict between the masses and the bureaucracy, the Al Ahram project sought to assess bureaucratic attitudes toward the Egyptian public. Just how do Egyptian bureaucrats view the masses? From the bureaucratic perspective, just how large is the gap between the two entities?

Four measures were used to examine the attitudes of the Egyptian bureaucrats toward the public they serve: (1) peer evaluations of bureaucratic behavior, (2) bureaucratic perceptions of the public, (3) bureaucratic explanations of the tensions that exist between the bureaucracy and the masses, and (4) an allocation of blame. Do bureaucrats believe that the root of the problem lies with the bureaucracy or with the masses?

Bureaucratic Evaluations of Bureaucratic Service

As an initial step in assessing the level of conflict between the bureaucracy and the masses, the respondents were requested to evaluate the quality of bureaucratic services. This step serves a dual purpose. First, it provides an empirical assessment of bureaucratic performance as viewed from the perspective of the bureaucrat. If bureaucrats rate themselves poorly in terms of their treatment of the masses, it may be safely assumed that their service to the masses is poor, indeed. Second, a poor self-assessment of bureaucratic service might provide some indication of the bureaucracy's willingness to acknowledge that bureaucratic treatment of the masses has been substandard. The more bureaucrats are willing to make such an acknowledgment, the easier it may be to modify their behavior. It is difficult to treat patients who deny that they are ill.

Four items contained in the group dynamics scale (Table 3.2) provide peer evaluations of bureaucratic service to the public. In these four items, respondents were requested to use Likert scale items to express the level of their agreement or disagreement with statements suggesting that their peers (1) treat the public with respect, (2) are more concerned with public service than job security, (3) listen to public opinions, and (4) solicit public opinions.

The questionnaire item suggesting that bureaucrats treat the public with respect resulted in a "strongly agree" rate of 26 percent, a figure indicating that respondents found little fault with bureaucratic behavior in this area.[4] There is little reason to judge this figure excessive, for as President Mubarak indicated in his address to the Parliament, one of the difficulties in dealing with the Egyptian bureaucracy is the tendency of most Egyptian bureaucrats to be superficially cooperative and to promise more than they can (or are willing to) deliver as a means of being polite and avoiding confrontation.[5]

The laudable figures for "treat the public with respect" drop rapidly in reference to the remaining items. Only 9.3 percent of the respondents "strongly agreed" that their colleagues listened to the view of the public, a figure that drops to 8.9 percent in terms of their willingness to solicit public opinions. The lowest of the four items and the lowest score on the group dynamics scale in general, was the meager 4.5 percent of the respondents who "strongly agreed" that their peers placed public service above concerns of job security. The job-security figure does not mean that Egyptian bureaucrats are unwilling to serve the public, but it does suggest that public service is not their primary concern.

In sum, the results of the peer evaluations support the general assumption that Egyptian bureaucrats tend to be insensitive to mass demands and are preoccupied by concerns of their own security and well-being. On the positive side, the results *may* indicate that the bureaucracy has not deluded itself into believing that its service to the public is satisfactory. If the results do indicate an awareness among bureaucrats that their performance is less than satisfactory, this awareness, of itself, may suggest a willingness by the bureaucracy to improve its public image. As later stages of the analysis will indicate, however, such a conclusion may not be justified.

Bureaucratic Perceptions of the Public

In assessing bureaucratic perceptions of the public, the Al Ahram project had two basic concerns. The first concern was to assess the self-perceived social status of Egyptian bureaucrats. Does the present generation of bureaucrats continue to believe that it enjoys the awesome respect that accrued to bureaucrats in decades past? The second concern was to ascertain the level of bureaucratic negativism toward the Egyptian public. Negativism breeds negativism. Indeed, the negativism and hostility on the part of even a minority of officials could well undermine the efforts of the majority. How negative, then, are bureaucratic perceptions of the masses?

Bureaucratic perceptions of bureaucratic status are important to the question of rapport between the masses and the bureaucracy inasmuch as they have a direct influence upon bureaucratic morale. Low morale does not bode well for a high level of bureaucratic service to the public. All things being equal, the morale of individuals in high-status occupations is likely to be far higher than the morale of individuals relegated to occupations on the lower rungs of the status hierarchy. This is even more the case among highly educated individuals living in a poorly educated society, not to mention individuals who believe themselves to be severely underpaid. Feelings of status deprivation do undermine morale. If present, they would offer at least a partial explanation of the intense apathy and low public concern manifested by Egyptian bureaucrats.

Bureaucratic perceptions of bureaucratic status in the public eye were assessed by two questionnaire items. The first item asked respondents to express their level of agreement with the statement that "the public respects civil servants." The second item asked respondents to assess the statement that "the public appreciates the efforts of civil servants." The results of both items are presented in Table 6.1. Collectively, they indicate a relatively low assessment of bureaucratic status. While 17 percent of the respondents did strongly agree with the statement that the public respects civil servants, this figure was judged by the research team to be a clear drop in prestige from the era of socialism and the monarchy. Particularly alarming, however, was the mere 7 percent of the population that felt that the efforts of the bureaucracy were appreciated by the masses.

Given the above results, there can be little doubt that it is

Table 6.1

Self-Perceptions of Bureaucratic Social Status
(n = 555)★

		Weighted★	Strongly Agree	
1.	The public respects civil servants.†	44	17.4%	(nr = 17)
2.	The public appreciated the efforts of civil servants.	22	7.2%	(nr = 14)

★Respondents not interacting with the public were not included in the calculations.

†Weighted scores represent a combination of "agree" and "strongly agree" responses in which the "strongly agree" responses have received twice the weight of "agree responses."

increasingly difficult for Egyptian bureaucrats to perceive themselves as members of a high-status profession. Moreover, when one combines the perceptions of declining occupational status with the abiding bureaucratic concern with prestige discussed in chapter 3, a strong case can be made for the argument that Egypt's bureaucrats do, indeed, suffer from acute feelings of status deprivation. Dismally paid and minimally appreciated, what is the incentive for Egypt's bureaucrats to improve their level of service to the masses? Perhaps more important, what is the incentive for Egypt's bureaucrats to provide the "doubled effort" called for in President Mubarak's 1985 speech to the Egyptian Parliament.[6]

Turning to bureaucratic negativism toward the masses, the Al Ahram project assessed three areas of mass/bureaucratic interaction: cooperation in providing information, honesty in dealing with the bureaucracy, and pressures for special treatment *(wasta)*. The results of these items appear in Table 6.2 and leave little doubt that one of the primary sources of tension between the bureaucracy and the masses from the bureaucratic perspective is the pervasive desire of the masses to acquire special treatment. Demands for *wasta,* among other things, disrupt the bureaucrat's routine. *Wasta* also requires the bureaucrat to expend personal "credits" with his peers and supervisors, credits that

Table 6.2

Bureaucratic Perceptions of the Egyptian Public
(n = 555)★

	Weighted score†	Strongly Agree Score
1. The public is cooperative in providing officials with information.	46	14.3%
		(nonresponse = 14)
2. People are honest in dealing with the bureaucracy.‡	29	10.4%
		(nonresponse = 18)
3. Most people are always trying to pull strings and get special treatment.	54	35.5%
		(nonresponse = 8)

★ Respondents not interacting with the public were deleted from the analysis.

† Starred items were presented in inverse order in the questionnaire.

‡ See explanation of weighting procedure on Table 6.1.

might be better spent for the bureaucrat's personal needs. Moreover, the more demands officials place upon their colleagues and supervisors to assist their friends and relatives, the more demands they must service in return and the more the tranquillity of their bureaucratic routine will be disrupted. In assessing the magnitude of this problem, one might recall the analysis of informal communication presented in chapter 4, an analysis which indicated that the foremost basis for interaction between the bureaucrats and their supervisors was the need for assistance in dealing with a government agency (Table 4.5).

Assessments of public honesty in dealing with the bureaucracy were also on the negative side, albeit far less so than concerns about *wasta*. Assessments of mass cooperation elicited little enthusiasm, yet the summary scores indicted that this was a matter of minor concern. As our panel of experts pointed out, the public has little choice but to provide government officials with minimal levels of cooperation and information if they hope to achieve their petitions. Bureaucrats, for better or worse, hold all of the cards.

Taken collectively, the three items relating to mass interaction reflect negativism toward the public, a negativism that does little to enhance the quality of the mass/bureaucratic relationship. Negativism toward the public, however, may be difficult to alter, for the major complaints of our respondents appear to be accurate reflections of mass behavior. If the bureaucracy reacts to the masses in an adversarial manner, it is not entirely without cause. Not only must the bureaucracy take the initiative in improving its relations with the masses, but it must do so in spite of less than total support from the masses.

Assessing the Causes of Mass/Bureaucratic Conflict

It is difficult to address the tension extant between the bureaucracy and the public without a clear understanding of its origin. Moreover, it is particularly important to know how the members of the bureaucracy perceive the problem, for, as noted above, it is the bureaucracy that must take the initiative in alleviating it.

As discussed at length in chapters 1 and 2, the causes of conflict between the bureaucracy and the public are many and varied. From a cultural or historical perspective, the conflict originated in the era of the monarchy, an era in which the bureaucracy ruled rather than served. As the role of the bureaucracy was largely to regulate and tax, tensions and distrust between the bureaucracy and the masses were to be expected.

Feelings of tension and distrust that found their origin in the era of the monarchy were further reinforced by the informal alliance between the political elites and the masses that evolved during the revolutionary era. The bureaucracy, in short, was made the scapegoat as both the Nasser and Sadat regimes found it impossible to achieve their social and developmental goals.

In the present era, conflict between the bureaucracy and the masses continues to be reinforced by the apathy, rigidity, and other dimensions of bureaucratic behavior discussed in the preceding chapters. So, too, is it reinforced by the ubiquitous red tape and routine that has become the hallmark of the Egyptian bureaucracy. To deal with the Egyptian bureaucracy is to be frustrated.

Finally, one must add mass behavior to the equation. The Egyptian public is relentless in seeking special favor. As a casual drive through Cairo's crowded thoroughfares will indicate, the average Egyptian does not score high on voluntary compliance with rules and regulations.[7] Aggravating, too, from the bureaucratic perspective, is the pervasive demand of Egyptians to go directly to the "boss," bypassing subordinate officials readily capable of addressing their problems.

While the causes of tension between the masses and bureaucracy are easily described, the critical question centers on the willingness and the ability of the government and the bureaucracy to take corrective measures. The Mubarak government, for its part, is keenly aware of the role of red tape in aggravating tensions between the bureaucracy and the masses and has embarked upon a program to simplify regulations and procedures, the simplification of procedures at the Cairo airport being a case in point.

While the government is cognizant of the need to improve trust and cooperation between the bureaucracy and the masses, it is not at all clear that the bureaucracy feels the same sense of urgency. This is a particularly critical issue, for it is the bureaucracy, when all is said and done, that must play the major role in recasting mass attitudes toward the bureaucracy.

The willingness of the bureaucracy to take the lead in recasting its relationship with the masses will depend in large measure upon the manner in which bureaucrats perceive the root causes of the problem. What, from the bureaucratic perspective, are the main causes of the tension between the bureaucracy and the masses?

Responses to this question are presented in Table 6.3 and have been divided into four basic categories: systemic problems, communications problems, mass behavior, and bureaucratic behavior. The data presented include both "first-choice" responses and the mean score of first-, second-, and third-choice responses.

Clearly the biggest problem area from the bureaucratic perspective was poor communication between the bureaucracy and the masses. The masses, in the bureaucratic eye, simply do not understand that the ability of the bureaucrat to facilitate their demands—legitimate and illegitimate—is circumscribed by the formal rigidity of

Table 6.3

Bureaucratic Explanations of Conflict between the Bureaucracy and the Public
(n = 555)*

Systemic Explanations	Mean Score†	First Choice
Public frustrated by red tape	11.4	18.6%
Impossible to help effectively	5.7	2.2
	17.1	20.8
Communications		
Public does not understand job of bureaucrat	19.4	52.8
Public does not understand role of bureaucrat	10.1	5.5
Public does not understand pressures of bureaucrat	3.1	.7
Mass demands unclear	7.2	5.3
	39.8	64.3
Mass Behavior		
Masses attempt to use influence	9.7	2.5
Masses impatient	5.7	.9
Masses avoid responsibilities	4.4	.6
Masses disobey rules	5.3	.9
Masses hostile	1.6	.3
	26.7	5.2
Bureaucratic Behavior		
Officials corrupt	3.9	1.5
Officials incompetent	3.3	1.5
Officials do not care about public	3.1	1.2
	10.3	4.2
Other		
No problems	3.8	3.7
Miscellaneous	2.0	2.8
	5.8%	6.5%

*Officials not interacting with the public were deleted from the analysis. Totals may vary from 100% owing to rounding error.

†The mean score represents the mean of the first, second, and third most important reasons for conflict between the bureaucracy and the masses.

the system, not to mention the behavioral rigidities resulting from the excessive concentration of authority and the unwillingness of most bureaucrats to assume unnecessary responsibilities. Contrary to mass expectations, average bureaucrats cannot do as they please. Indeed a large share of the structural rigidity within the Egyptian bureaucracy is the result of procedures instituted to prevent officials from granting special favors (and other forms of corruption). The results of this situation are twofold. First, the masses are resentful because their petitions have been denied or delayed by bureaucrats whom they believe could have done otherwise had they so desired. Second, as the results illustrate, the bureaucrats are frustrated by the enormity of mass demands that they either cannot facilitate or that they cannot facilitate without more effort or risk than they care to expend.

The communication category was distinguished from the mass behavior category on the logic that communication problems convey far less hostility on the part of bureaucrats than do the accusations of mass maleficence implied by the mass behavior items. Moreover, problems of communication are, presumably, more amenable to change than deeply set behavioral problems. It is encouraging, accordingly, that the majority of the bureaucrats surveyed did not manifest overt hostility toward the masses.

The mass behavior category, however, was far from negligible. A full 26 percent of those respondents who interacted with the masses blamed the poor rapport between the bureaucracy and the masses on items such as mass demands for *wasta,* mass hostility, mass avoidance of responsibility, mass violation of rules, or mass pushiness. The more bureaucrats harbor negative perceptions of the masses, the less likely they are to walk the extra mile needed to generate greater understanding and cooperation between themselves and their clients. The willingness to walk the extra mile is particularly important, for as stressed above, it is incumbent upon the bureaucracy to take the lead in improving their relations with the Egyptian public. It is the bureaucracy that must rekindle the masses' faith in its ability to solve Egypt's dire economic and social problems.

Viewed in this light, the most disappointing aspect of this phase of the analysis was the reluctance of our respondents to acknowledge bureaucratic behavior as a major source of tension between the bureaucracy and the masses. As indicated in Table 6.3, only 4.2 percent of the respondents cited bureaucratic corruption, incompetence, and apathy as their first-choice explanation of mass/bureaucratic conflict. Even worse, only 10 percent of the sample listed bureaucratic behavior as one of three causes of the problem.

Also of some interest was the relatively low tendency of the respondents to list bureaucratic red tape as the source of tensions between the bureaucracy and the mass. While red tape did garner 18.6 percent of the first-choice scores, it nevertheless faded to 11 percent of the averaged responses across the three choices, finishing a poor third to mass behavior problems and communications problems. This finding, in conjunction with the low score on the bureaucratic behavior items, manifests a clear propensity on the part of the bureaucrats to place the blame for any conflict between the bureaucracy and the masses squarely on the shoulders of the masses. It also suggests that the average bureaucrat does not see the need to markedly rethink his or her own attitudes toward the masses.

Who is to Blame?

At an earlier point in the analysis it was suggested that the respondents' acknowledgment that their treatment of the masses was sub-par might well be interpreted as a positive sign of their willingness to make a concerted effort to improve their service to the public. At the very least, it was suggested that such an awareness might be considered as the first step in designing a solution to the problem on the grounds that it is difficult to solve problems that are not acknowledged. As we have seen, however, bureaucratic explanations of the poor rapport between the bureaucracy and the masses cast serious doubt upon this theory.

In order to bring the question of bureaucratic attitudes toward the masses into clearer focus, respondents were explicitly asked to indicate which party they felt was responsible for the tension between the two entities, the masses or the bureaucracy. The results of this item are presented in Table 6.4 and indicate that 75.6 percent of the respondents felt that the masses were primarily responsible for the problem. In spite of acknowledgments that its own behavior toward the masses is flawed, it is doubtful that the bureaucracy is predisposed to take the first step in improving relations with the Egyptian public.

Table 6.4

Who Is to Blame?

Mass is the problem	75.6%
Bureaucracy is the problem	24.4

n = 555 (Respondents not interacting with the public were deleted from the total "n" of 796.)

nonresponse = 3

Summary and Conclusion

Enhancement of Egypt's bureaucratic capacity is inextricably linked to the level of cooperation and trust extant between the bureaucracy and the masses. Indeed, former Prime Minister Lutfi listed improved cooperation between the masses and the government as the first of ten steps required to achieve Egypt's goal of sustained economic growth. The bureaucracy must, of necessity, take the lead in improving levels of trust, confidence, and cooperation between the masses and the diverse agencies of the Egyptian government.

A peer assessment of bureaucratic behavior vis-à-vis the masses supported general perceptions that the Egyptian bureaucracy was not overly responsive to either the needs or the views of the Egyptian masses. Added to this finding were the results of parallel questionnaire items suggesting that the bureaucracy was generally negative in its perceptions of the masses. In particular, the bureaucracy was frustrated by pervasive mass demands for *wasta*. These findings, of themselves, suggest that the bureaucracy may be less than willing to either initiate or sustain a program of improved public relations.

Two additional findings strongly support this view. First, it was strikingly evident that the majority of the bureaucrats surveyed severely underevaluate the role of bureaucratic behavior as a factor shaping the lack of rapport and trust between the bureaucracy and the masses. They placed the blame squarely on the masses. If the fault lies with the masses, what can the bureaucracy do? Second, the data suggests that the bureaucracy suffers from feelings of status deprivation. It is truly unlikely that a marked improvement in mass/bureaucracy relations will occur unless the government addresses the problems of bureaucratic morale analyzed in chapter 3.

7

✍

The Attributes of Bureaucratic Performance

Chapters 3 through 6 examined four behavioral components of bureaucratic capacity: productivity, flexibility, innovation, and relations with the public. The objective of this chapter is to examine the correlates of these components. In particular, we will address three basic questions: (1) which areas of the Egyptian bureaucracy rank highest in terms of behavioral capacity? (2) what factors are associated with higher levels of behavioral capacity? and (3) how can behavioral capacity be strengthened? Toward this end, the questionnaire items and scales used in the earlier stages of the analysis were correlated with a variety of independent variables hypothesized to influence bureaucratic performance including: job unit, job level, education, training, age, sex, recruitment, place of birth, religion, morale, media habits, reference groups, group dynamics, supervisor dynamics, and systemic support. Income proved to be a reflection of job level and was dropped from the analysis. The results of the cross tabulations are presented in summary form and include only those results that were significant to at least the .05 level and in which the strength of the relationship exceeded a Gamma coefficient of plus or minus .200.[1] The results of cross tabulations not meeting this standard are of negligible importance and have not been reported.

The following indicators of behavioral capacity will be used in this stage of the analysis:

1. Productivity. Productivity was measured by four indicators. The first indicator was based upon job satisfaction. Individuals who found their greatest source of job satisfaction in professional growth and development were assumed to be more productive than individuals that found their greatest satisfaction in nonprofessional areas such

121

as chatting with their peers. This indicator of performance is based upon the work of Herzberg and was discussed at length in chapter 3.[2]

The second measure of productivity was based upon sources of professional information. In this regard, it was assumed that individuals who took the time and effort to consult professional materials in the execution of their job responsibilities would be more productive than individuals who relied on other members of the work unit for their professional information. The percentage distributions for this indicator are to be found in Table 3.3. The third indicator of productivity was based upon the work-value index (Table 3.7) and distinguishes between individuals who placed greater and lesser emphasis upon job comfort and job ease. Individuals primarily concerned with the comfort and ease of their positions were judged to be less productive than individuals willing to expend greater effort for the sake of money, prestige, or other values. The value indicator of productivity is applicable only to the lower and middle levels of bureaucracy. The percentage distributions for the value-based indicator of productivity are also provided in Table 3.3.

The final evaluation of productivity is based upon peer evaluations of hard work (Table 3.2).

2. Flexibility was measured by three indicators, the first of which was the willingness of senior officials to delegate authority. This indicator applies only to senior-level officials and was based upon the results of item 2 in Table 4.1. The second indicator is based upon the extent to which middle- and lower-level officials were willing to bend the rules for the sake of greater efficiency (Table 4.3). The third indicator is based upon the group dynamics scale, with particular reference to items evaluating the willingness of peers to accept new responsibilities, to take risks, and to be flexible in the execution of decisions (Table 3.2).

3. Innovation was measured by three indicators: the social predisposition toward innovation items (Table 5.2), the decision-making innovation items and scale (Table 5.3), and the group dynamics item relating to a willingness to accept new ideas (Table 3.2).

4. Mass regarding was based upon four indicators: (1) the extent to which officials felt they were appreciated by the masses (Table 6.1), the extent that officials felt the masses were cooperative (Table 6.2), the extent that officials placed the blame for poor rapport between the bureaucracy and the masses on the masses (Table 6.4),

and finally, peer evaluations of bureaucratic sensitivity to mass opinions (Table 3.2).

Job Unit and Bureaucratic Capacity

It is a truism to say that some bureaucratic units are more productive than others. The crucial question from the perspective of the Egyptian bureaucracy is the extent to which the more productive units can serve as a model for increasing the productivity of the system as a whole. Technology transferred from within the Egyptian bureaucracy is far more likely to be effective in the Egyptian context than technology imported from the radically different environments of the United States, Western Europe, or the Soviet Union.

In order to provide a general idea of performance differences within the Egyptian bureaucracy, the Al Ahram study focused upon three diverse bureaucratic units: the welfare-oriented Ministry of Social Affairs, the production-oriented Ministry of Industry, and the Aluminum Corporation, a public corporation reputed to be among the most productive of Egypt's public corporations. Because the Aluminum Corporation was reputed to be more productive than either the Ministries of Industry or Social Affairs, it was hypothesized that the officials of the Aluminum Corporation would score higher on all of the behavioral indicators of bureaucratic capacity than their counterparts in the mainline ministries. A second hypothesis suggested that the production orientation of the Ministry of Industry would result in its officials scoring higher on the behavioral indicators of developmental capacity than the officials of the Ministry of Social Affairs. The logic in this hypothesis was that the Ministry of Industry would be more closely tied to specific production goals than the Ministry of Social Affairs.

1. Job unit and productivity. The hypothesis that officials in the Aluminum Corporation would be more productive than officials in the mainline ministries was supported by both the job-satisfaction indicator of productivity ($g = .222$) and the professional-reference indicator of productivity ($g = .258$). Officials in the Aluminum Corporation also were less inclined to view their peers as lazy ($g = .324$). On the negative side, lower-level officials at the Aluminum Corpora-

tion were more inclined to value comfort and security than their counterparts in the Ministries of Industry and Social Affairs.

2. Job unit and flexibility. The hypothesis that officials of the Aluminum Corporation would be more flexible in the delegation of authority and in the assumption of new responsibility than their counterparts in the mainline ministries was not sustained. To the contrary, senior officials in the Aluminum Corporation were among the most avid centralizers of authority in the Egyptian bureaucracy ($g = .562$).

In terms of peer evaluations, officials of the Aluminum Corporation found their colleagues to be more receptive to new responsibilities than did officials in the mainline ministries ($g = .241$). By the same token, however, officials of the Aluminum Corporation were judged to be somewhat less willing to take risks ($g = .202$).

3. Job unit and innovation. The hypothesis that officials in the Aluminum Corporation would be more innovative than officials in the Ministries of Industry and Social Affairs was not sustained. Officials of the Aluminum Corporation did, however, rank their peers higher in willingness to try new ideas than officials in the comparison units ($g = .486$).

4. Job unit and mass regarding. The hypothesis that officials in the Aluminum Corporation would be more mass oriented than their counterparts in the other units was not sustained. If anything, officials of the Aluminum Corporation felt less appreciated by the masses than officials in the comparison units ($g = .201$). They were also more likely to place the blame for poor rapport between the mass and the bureaucracy on the masses ($g = .258$).[3]

Differences in bureaucratic behavior between officials of the Ministry of Industry and officials of the Ministry of Social Affairs were minimal, the major difference being a far greater tendency for officials in the Ministry of Social Affairs to consult the rule book as a basis for decision making ($g = .421$). As officials in the Ministry of Social Welfare have far more contact with the public than officials in the Ministry of Industry, this finding supports the discussion in chapter 2 suggesting that bureaucrats use the rigidity of bureaucratic rules to shield themselves from the demands of the public.[4]

In summary, then, the officials of the Aluminum Corporation did appear to be more productive than officials in the Ministries of Industry and Social Affairs. They did not, however, rank higher than their mainline counterparts in terms of flexibility, innovativeness, or mass regarding. Indeed, the Aluminum Corporation ranked the lowest of the three groups in terms of the willingness of their senior officials to delegate authority. Perhaps authoritarian leadership is more conducive to productivity in the Egyptian environment than it is in the Western bureaucratic environment! The theory is clearly worthy of further investigation.

What, then, explains the greater productivity of the Aluminum Corporation? And, perhaps more important, does the experience of the Aluminum Corporation provide a guide for improving productivity throughout the Egyptian bureaucracy?

In an effort to answer these questions, job unit was correlated with several explanatory variables believed by the respondents and interviewees to influence the quality of bureaucratic behavior. Prominent in the list of explanatory variables were the following: incentive values, morale, recruitment, training, and demographics. This stage of the analysis produced some interesting differences between the Aluminum Corporation on one hand and the Ministries of Industry and Social Affairs on the other. The behavior of officials at the Aluminum Corporation (listed in summary form below) differed from the behavior of officials in the Ministries of Industry and Social Affairs in the following areas:

1. They were more likely to have received their positions by *wasta* and less likely to have received their positions via graduation.[5]
2. They were more likely to be working in the unit of their choice ($g = .418$).
3. They were more likely to be working in close proximity to relatives ($g = .672$).
4. They were more likely to communicate openly with their supervisors on both personal ($g = .288$) and work–related matters ($g = .222$).
5. They were far more likely to receive early promotions or to be promoted on schedule ($g = .335$) and to believe that the promotions were fair ($g = .528$).
6. They were more optimistic about future improvement in their standard of living ($g = .256$).
7. In general, they were more positive about the performance of their peers.
8. Demographically, they were primarily male ($g = .777$) and were drawn largely from the rural areas ($g = .658$).

9. Their work values showed a greater willingness to work in the rural areas for the sake of more money and other values, a finding reflecting the rural location of the Aluminum Corporation.

Taken as a whole, the differences between the officials of the Aluminum Corporation and their counterparts in the Ministries of Industry and Social Affairs fall roughly into two categories: demographic differences and differences in morale. Demographic differences tend to be an artifact of the location of the Aluminum Corporation and are not readily transferable from one unit to another. The antipathy of Cairines to jobs outside of the Cairo metroplex, however, should not be ignored. Indeed, it is very relevant to government plans for greater decentralization of the bureaucracy. Productivity in units located outside of Cairo (or Alexandria) will probably be more productive if the officials of such units are recruited locally.

Morale-based differences between the Aluminum Corporation and the mainline ministries, by contrast, would appear to be transferable. The superior morale of officials at the Aluminum Corporation was manifested in several ways: they were more positive in evaluating the work habits of their peers, thereby suggesting a more positive group environment. They enjoyed better communications with their supervisors, and, in sharp contrast to officials in the comparison groups, they were promoted on time and they felt that the promotion system was fair. Matters of promotion, in particular, should be relatively easy to improve on a system-wide basis.

While improvements in morale are desirable on their own merits, the link between morale and productivity is ambiguous. Exceptionally low morale may depress productivity. Improving morale by increasing salaries alone, however, may have minimal influence on productivity. Promotions, by contrast, add an important prestige component to the incentive process. As such, they address the predominant incentive value of the Egyptian bureaucracy. The theoretical background and data pertinent to this argument are to be found in chapter 3.

Education and Bureaucratic Capacity

The senior officials participating in the Al Ahram project attributed a lion's share of Egypt's bureaucratic malaise to the low skill levels of their employees. If this assessment is correct, it means that strengthening the behavioral capacity of the Egyptian bureaucracy involves little more than increased training in skill areas such as typing, computers, and accounting. As appealing as this argument may be, it is easy to overstate the importance of education and training as the cause of Egypt's bureaucratic woes. Education is not a panacea that can work miracles in the face of adverse environmental, cultural, and systemic circumstances. It should also be recalled that the Egyptian bureaucracy already represents a highly educated strata of Egyptian society, with some 53 percent of the respondents possessing college experience.

Accepting the view of the senior bureaucrats, it was hypothesized that each of the behavioral dimensions of bureaucratic capacity would improve with education and training. Three indicators of education were used in the analysis: education level, participation in local in-service training programs, and participation in foreign training programs.

1. Education level and productivity. Correlations between education level and the job-satisfaction indicator of productivity supported the hypothesis that productivity increased with education level, but only moderately so ($g = .277$). Foreign training programs were also positively related with productivity, but less so than education level ($g = .241$). Local training programs had no impact on this specific indicator of productivity.

The professional-reference indicator of productivity provided support for the link between education and productivity ($g = .517$). Again, however, the impact of training programs on productivity was less than that of general education, with foreign programs having greater impact on productivity ($g = .410$) than local training programs ($g = .278$).

The work-value measure of productivity also increased with education ($g = .236$) but was unrelated to either local or foreign training programs.

Peer evaluations of productivity were not influenced by educational experience.

The finding that education level had a greater impact upon productivity than either foreign or local training programs raises the possibility that the correlations between in-service training programs and productivity were merely an artifact of the strong correlation between education level and participation in both local training programs ($g = .467$) and foreign training programs ($g = .686$). In order to explore this relationship further, the cross tabulations between training programs and productivity were controlled for education level. The results of the control procedures indicate that training programs contribute only modestly to the productivity of poorly educated workers and add virtually nothing to productivity levels of bureaucrats with secondary or higher levels of education. One must conclude, accordingly, that training programs had little independent impact on productivity. Moreover, the data also indicate that the most productive officials are no more likely to participate in training programs than their less-productive peers. Actually, there was some suggestion that productive individuals were less likely to be selected for training programs than their peers (g = .235).

2. Education and flexibility. The hypothesis that the predisposition of supervisors to delegate authority and the corresponding predisposition of subordinates to assume responsibility would increase with education and training was not sustained. This result supports our earlier suggestion (chapter 4) that the rigidity of the Egyptian bureaucracy is deeply rooted in Egyptian cultural values and may be very difficult to alter by means of training and educational programs.

3. Innovation and education. The hypothesis that innovation increased with education and training was supported with reference to decision-making innovation. In this regard, both dependence upon supervisors and tendencies to delay decisions for fear of making mistakes decreased with education level. The relevant coefficients were (g = .384) and (g = .305), respectively. The correlation between the decision-making innovation scale and education level was (g = .305). Foreign training programs followed essentially the same pattern. Local training programs had minimal influence on decision-making innovation.

Turning to social innovation, one finds a slightly greater willingness on the part of educated officials to support programs that risk social conflict (g = .201). Educated officials were also slightly more supportive of Western values than their less well educated peers (g = .207). The impact of education upon social innovation, however, is substantially less than its influence upon decision-making innovation (g = .302), a result also indicating the limited utility of education as a means of altering deeply rooted cultural values. Training programs had no discernible impact upon the predispositions toward social innovation.

4. Education and mass regarding. The hypothesis that rapport

with the masses increased with education received very little support. Indeed, the only discernible influence of education on the various dimensions of mass regarding analyzed in chapter 6 was a somewhat greater tendency of educated officials to feel appreciated and respected by the masses. The coefficients were (g = .239) and (g = .217), respectively. Training programs had little impact upon attitudes toward the masses, the sole exception being a slight tendency for local training programs to reinforce feelings that the poor rapport between the bureaucracy and the masses was largely the fault of the masses.

In summarizing the influence of education and training upon behavioral capacity, several conclusions would appear to be in order. First, education level does make a difference in the critical areas of productivity and decision-making innovation, areas that tend to be skill oriented and that are minimally influenced by broader cultural influences. Social innovation, flexibility, and mass regarding, by contrast, appear to be rooted in prevailing cultural norms and were minimally influenced by education and training. Be this as it may, it is also clear that education and training do not provide the panacea for bureaucratic development envisioned in the responses of the senior administrators. Education may be a necessary condition for improving bureaucratic capacity, but it is not a sufficient condition. Also relevant to this point was the minimal impact of training programs upon the various dimensions of bureaucratic capacity. This was particularly true of local training programs. A thorough review of the scope, content, procedures, and objectives of local training programs may well be in order. Also in order is a review of the selection procedures for all training programs and for foreign training programs in particular. It is not at all clear that the most productive individuals are being provided with the opportunity to improve and extend their professional credentials.

Job Level

If the behavioral capacity of a bureaucracy is a function of productivity, flexibility, innovation, and rapport with the masses, it is also a function of how well these attributes are distributed throughout the various levels of the bureaucracy. Greater productivity, flexibility, and innovation at the senior level of the bureaucracy, for example, may lead to little more than the frustration of senior officials if they are not reciprocated at the middle and lower levels of the bureaucracy. By the same token, the desire of lower- and middle-level bureaucrats for greater responsibility and innovation in their daily operations could well be stymied by the inflexibility of their superiors. How evenly then are the attributes of productivity, flexibility, innovation, and mass rapport distributed among the three basic levels of the Egyptian bureaucracy?

The answer to this question was approached by cross tabulating job level with the various indicators of bureaucratic capacity. In line with the views of our consultants, it was hypothesized that the strength of the bureaucracy would lie with its upper-level officials.

1. Job level and productivity. The job-satisfaction, professional-reference, and work-value indicators of productivity all found productivity to increase with job level. The coefficients were ($g = .215$), ($g = .403$), and ($g = .242$), respectively. The coefficients are somewhat deceptive, however, for they mask the tendency of middle-level bureaucrats to be at least if not more productive than their superiors. This was clearly the case in regard to the professional-reference indicator of productivity. Expressed in percentage terms, 15.4 percent of the middle-level officials referred to professional materials in the execution of their responsibilities as opposed to 8.6 percent of the senior officials and only 1.9 percent of the lower-level officials. The percentages for the job-satisfaction indicator of productivity were more balanced with 36.7 percent of the senior officials falling into the most productive category as opposed to 33.4 percent and 23 percent of the middle- and lower-level officials, respectively. In terms of the value-based indicator of productivity, 16.5 percent of the middle-level officials fell in the productive category as opposed to only 9 percent of the lower-level officials. We shall return to this theme in the discussion of age and productivity. For the present, suffice it to say that the lower level of the Egyptian bureaucracy is clearly the least productive.

2. Job level and flexibility. The indicators of flexibility were tailored to job level and precluded comparisons across the three levels of authority. Differences in flexibility did not occur between the middle and lower levels.

3. Job level and innovation. Senior and middle-level bureaucrats scored significantly higher on the decision-making innovation scale than did their lower-level subordinates ($g = .439$). In particular, middle- and upper-level officials were far less inclined to clear all issues with their superiors or to delay nonroutine decisions than were lower-level officials. Expressed in percentage terms, all of the high inno-

vators (1.3%) were in the upper level of the bureaucracy. Twenty-four percent of the senior bureaucrats were in the moderately innovative category in contrast to 14 percent of the middle-level and 7.2 percent of the lower-level bureaucrats. Apparently only the upper-level bureaucrats feel free to spread their wings and try new ideas, a phenomenon clearly reflecting the rigid deference patterns within the bureaucracy.

Aside from a slightly greater receptivity of upper-level officials toward Western values ($g = .261$), predispositions toward social innovation were relatively uniform across the three levels.

4. Job level and mass regarding. With the exception of a slightly greater tendency for upper-level officials to perceive themselves as respected by the masses, the hypothesis that concern for mass rapport would increase with job level was not sustained.

In summary, both productivity and decision-making innovation are concentrated in the upper and middle levels of the bureaucracy. It is entirely possible, accordingly, that much of the drive and innovation that do exist within the Egyptian bureaucracy are blunted by the far lower productivity of the lower echelons of the bureaucracy, echelons entrusted with the execution of programs emanating from on high. Various consultants also suggested that the Egyptian penchant for overplanning (and concentration of authority) may be the direct result of senior officials attempting to compensate for the lower productivity and inferior skill levels among their subordinates. In this view, detailed plans and authoritarianism are the only way to get things accomplished. Be this as it may, the rigidity of the Egyptian bureaucracy remains one of its greatest weaknesses. Using structural mechanisms to solve behavioral problems often creates more problems than it solves. Authoritarianism by supervisors also reinforces passiveness in the lower ranks of the bureaucracy. Finally, it should be noted that the senior bureaucrats appear to provide little incentive toward improving rapport with the masses.

Age

The relationship between age and bureaucratic behavior submits to two contrary hypotheses. The first hypothesis suggests that productivity, innovation, and the other attributes of behavioral capacity increase as the individual matures and gains in skill, confidence, and the knowledge of how best to accomplish tasks within the constraints of the bureaucratic system. The second hypothesis suggests that younger bureaucrats may be better educated and have greater exposure to Western values than older bureaucrats. They also have less time to be ground down by the system. As such, they should rank higher in the various indices of behavioral capacity.

Given the earlier finding that several dimensions of bureaucratic capacity increased with job level, it was hypothesized that correlations between age and bureaucratic capacity would follow the same pattern. The correlation coefficient between age and job level, by way of reference, was (g = .735). The picture, however, is not as clear as it might be. The correlations between age and productivity were of a lower order than the corresponding correlations between the job level and productivity. The same was true of correlations between age and decision-making innovation.

The relatively weak correlations between age on one hand and productivity on the other, are the result of the curvilinear nature of the relationship between the two variables. Productivity does increase with age but only up to a point. Productivity tapers off among older officials. Also interesting was the tendency for productivity to be highest in the thirty-nine to fifty-five age range for upper-level officials but to shift to younger employees at the middle and lower levels. Roughly the same pattern existed in the cross tabulations between age and decision-making innovation. This would suggest that older employees at the junior levels have been passed over for promotion and that they have lost interest in their work. In line with the earlier discussion of flexibility and job level, it also suggests that the role and status of productive officials located in the middle and lower levels of the bureaucracy are particularly worthy of study. Are productivity and innovation being rewarded? Or, to the contrary, do more productive and innovative officials in the junior levels of the bureaucracy find their efforts suffocated by the authoritarianism of their superiors? Is the Egyptian bureaucracy making the most of the productive officials located in its lower ranks?

Sex

The relationship between sex and bureaucratic behavior became a question of considerable interest in the mid- and late 1970s, a period that witnessed an increase in the number of females entering the bureaucracy via the graduates policy and the simultaneous migration of male bureaucrats to the oil states and the private sector. Indeed, it was during this period that people began to speculate about the feminization of the Egyptian bureaucracy and its impact on bureaucratic performance.[6]

How, then, do female officials compare with their male counterparts in terms of the four dimensions of behavioral capacity? Will the expanding role of female bureaucrats decrease the developmental capacity of the bureaucracy, as some of our informal interviews suggested, or will the expanding role of females prove to be its salvation?

The answer, alas, appears to be neither. The female respondents ranked neither higher nor lower than their male counterparts in terms of the four dimensions of behavioral capacity. The only exception to this statement was a slight tendency for males to be more productive in terms of the professional-reference indicator of productivity. Females, however, did differ markedly from males in terms of their work values, a subject to be examined at length in chapter 3.[7]

Media Preference and Bureaucratic Capacity

It has long been an axiom of developmental theory that exposure to Western mass media introduces and reinforces modern values among Third World populations.[8] As the various attributes of bureaucratic behavior examined in the Al Ahram study are manifestations of "modern" behavior, it was hypothesized that productivity, innovation, flexibility, and mass regarding would be positively correlated with exposure to Western media.[9] It was similarly hypothesized that individuals ranking high in the various attributes of bureaucratic capacity would prefer political and economic media programming to programming that stressed entertainment or traditional cultural values. The logic of this hypothesis was that political and economic programming is change oriented and stresses awareness of Egypt's myriad economic and social problems, the solutions of which ultimately rest with the Egyptian bureaucracy.

In order to examine the influence of the mass media upon bureaucratic behavior, the respondents were presented with a variety of questionnaire items relating to their media habits and preferences,

Table 7.1

Media Habits of Egyptian Bureaucrats

(n = 796)

How many times a week do you read a newspaper?

Daily	76.4	
Several	18.2	
Once or twice	4.9	
Less	.5	
	100%★	(nonresponse = 3)

How many times a week do you read magazines?

Daily	7.3	
Several	45.2	
Once or twice	36.1	
Less	11.4	
	100%	(nonresponse = 16)

How often do you listen to the radio?

Daily	55.5	
Several	28.3	
Once or twice	9.7	
Less	6.4	
	100%	(nonresponse = 4)

How often do you watch T.V.?

Daily	65.4	
Several	26.1	
Once or twice	5.4	
Less	3.1	
	100%	(nonresponse = 2)

In general, do you prefer foreign or local papers?

Local	89.2	

Table 7.1
(continued)

Foreign	1.0
Both	9.8
	100%

(nonresponse = 6)

Do you prefer local or foreign radio?

Local	62.1
Foreign	4.8
Both	33.1
	100%

(nonresponse = 29)

Which sections of the newspaper do you prefer? (first choice)

Fortune telling	2.5
T.V. schedule	19.1
Cultural	20.0
Politics/news	25.4
Economics	8.9
Social	18.2
Other	5.9
	100%

(nonresponse = 9)

Which radio programs do you prefer? (first choice)

News	40.1
Culture	15.2
Politics	4.3
Music	14.4
Drama	4.3
Sports	3.1
Quran	15.1
Other	3.4

(nonresponse = 32)

Which T.V. programs do you prefer? (first choice)

News	31.2

Table 7.1
(continued)

Culture	14.9
Politics	2.4
Music	5.3
Drama/films	24.0
Sports	9.1
Quran	11.0
Other	2.1
	100% (nonresponse = 3)

Combined foreign media exposure

Local only	59.8
Low foreign	27.9
High foreign	10.7
Foreign only	1.8
	100%

*Totals may vary from 100% owing to rounding error.

the text and percentage distributions for which appear in Table 7.1. The data thus presented suggest three basic conclusions:

1. Egyptian bureaucrats are intense consumers of the mass media in all of its forms.

2. Egyptian bureaucrats are locally oriented in their media consumption, a fact that may go a long way toward explaining the pervasiveness of general cultural values and mores among Egyptian bureaucrats in spite of their high level of education and special status within Egyptian society. It will be noted in Table 7.1, for example, that approximately 60 percent of the Egyptian officials have virtually no exposure to the foreign media.

3. Egyptian bureaucrats are clearly oriented toward cultural and entertainment programming as opposed to change-oriented political and economic analysis, a finding which reinforces the link between bureaucratic behavior and general culture mores.

The relationship between media behavior and behavioral capacity centers on three basic hypotheses: (1) behavioral capacity increases with media exposure regardless of its origin or content, (2) bureaucratic capacity increases with exposure to foreign media, and (3) bureaucratic capacity increases with the social-change orientation of media preferences.

Media Consumption and Behavioral Capacity. The intense media consumption manifested by all of the respondents made it impossible to test the hypothesis that bureaucratic capacity increased with total media consumption. There were simply too few nonconsumers to make the correlations meaningful.

Foreign Media and Behavioral Capacity. The hypothesis that bureaucratic capacity would increase with exposure to foreign media received support only in the areas of productivity and decision-making innovation. Specifically, the correlation between the professional-reference indicator of productivity and foreign media exposure was $(g = .243)$, with the corresponding coefficient for total media exposure being $(g = .221)$. The remaining indicators of productivity were not influenced by exposure to foreign media.

The relationship between exposure to the foreign press and decision-making innovation was considerably stronger, achieving a coefficient of $(g = .399)$. Corresponding coefficients for foreign radio exposure and total exposure to foreign media were $(g = .239)$ and $(g = .239)$ and $(g = .273)$, respectively.

Media Content and Behavioral Capacity. The hypothesis that the various dimensions of behavioral capacity would be influenced by content preference was supported only in reference to decision-making innovation. In this regard, individuals expressing a preference for economic and political analysis did manifest a greater propensity for innovative decision making than individuals preferring cultural or entertainment-oriented programming. The gamma coefficients for the correlations between economic content and innovation and political content and innovation were $(g = .255)$ and $(g = .215)$, respectively.

The finding that productivity and decision-making innovation were at least marginally influenced by various dimensions of media exposure is relevant to the analysis in at least two regards. First, it suggests that productivity and innovation might be enhanced by making both officials and trainees more aware of the critical link between bureaucratic behavior and the broader goals of social and economic development. Second, media consumption items might find a role in screening profiles designed to identify the more productive members of the Egyptian bureaucracy.

Perhaps of greater relevance than the marginal influence of media behavior on decision-making innovation and the professional-reference indicator of productivity was the almost total lack of media influence on the other dimensions of bureaucratic capacity including the job-satisfaction and value-based indicators of productivity. The clear preference of Egyptian bureaucrats for local programming highlights the local orientation of the Egyptian bureaucracy. Concern for foreign opinions and bureaucratic role models appears to be minimal.

This point was also graphically illustrated by the results of reference group items requesting the respondents to indicate the sources of information that they found most useful in shaping their economic and professional decisions. As indicated in Table 7.2, less than 8 percent of the respondents used the foreign media as a primary source of economic information, with less than 1 percent of the respondents finding the foreign media to be a primary source of administrative information. Twenty-four percent of the respondents, by way of contrast, listed the local media as a primary source of economic information, with 4.3 percent listing the Egyptian media as a primary source of administrative information. Although Egyptian officials may be avid consumers of the mass media, they are not using the media as a source of administrative information. Rather, it would appear that their intense consumption of the local media serves to reinforce the link between bureaucratic culture and Egyptian culture in general. This cultural link, it will be recalled, was particularly relevant in explaining the rigidity of the Egyptian bureaucracy as well as its adherence to traditional social values.

Group Dynamics

Western studies of public administration have long stressed the link between the group environment and individual productivity.[10] It would seem natural, accordingly, to hypothesize that behavioral capacity would also be directly influenced by the group environment. The group dynamics scale introduced in chapter 3 (Table 3.2) provided the opportunity to examine the extent to which the group

Table 7.2

Information Reference Sources
(n = 796)

What sources of information do you find most useful in making economic decisions?

	First Choice	Second Choice
Colleagues	28.3%	9.0%
Notables	14.0	13.6
Egyptian media	31.7	16.4
Arab media	1.5	4.4
Foreign media	4.8	10.7
Political parties	1.3	2.8
Friends/relatives	7.3	19.6
Professional materials	10.4	21.8
Other	.6	1.6
	100%	100%

nonresponse = 1,3

What sources of information do you find most useful in making decisions related to your job?

	First Choice	Second Choice
Colleagues	34.1	12.1
Notables	8.8	6.8
Egyptian media	4.4	4.2
Arab media	.9	1.8
Foreign media	.6	.9
Political parties	2.6	5.0
Friends/relatives	5.7	9.3
Professional materials	17.6	17.2
Rules and manuals	16.7	24.2
Supervisor	8.6	18.5
	100%	100%

nonresponse = 0,2

139

environment of the Egyptian bureaucracy influenced the various indicators of behavioral capacity. Specifically, it was hypothesized that the more individuals ranked their peers high in terms of performance, the more they would feel that they were working in a professionally stimulating environment and, ipso facto, the higher they would score in terms of the various dimensions of behavioral capacity.

In order to test this hypothesis, the sixteen items composing the group dynamics scale were cross tabulated with the various indicators of bureaucratic capacity. The results of the cross tabulations failed to sustain the hypothesis. Indeed, the few correlation coefficients to meet the criteria of significance and strength indicated that group environment was inversely related to bureaucratic capacity. The two major examples of this phenomenon were the tendency of individuals ranking high on the decision-making innovation scale to view their peers as lazy (g = .218) and a corresponding tendency of individuals with a positive attitude toward the masses to find their peers to be unwilling to receive new responsibility (g = .251), to be indecisive (g = .228), and to be reluctant to discuss community problems with the public (g = .200). While the above data is limited in scope, it does suggest that group dynamics within the Egyptian bureaucracy depress rather than stimulate professional behavior. The topic clearly demands additional study.

Supervisor Dynamics

Relations between supervisors and subordinates have also been a major focal point of Western studies of motivation and productivity.[11] In particular, both the openness of supervisor-subordinate relations and the positive reinforcement of subordinates by supervisors have been cited as major factors improving productivity in the Western bureaucratic setting. It was hypothesized, accordingly, that both the open interaction of supervisors and subordinates and the positive reinforcement of subordinates by supervisors would also be related to increased behavioral capacity among Egyptian officials.

The openness of superior-subordinate relationships in the Egyptian bureaucracy was reviewed in chapter 4 and was found to be limited in scope and formal in nature. The impact of open communi-

Table 7.3

Positive Reinforcement

Do you believe that your supervisor tells the people above that you are a good worker? (middle and lower levels)

Frequently	15.4%
Occasionally	40.6
Does not praise people	6.3
Complains	1.4
Do not know	36.4
	100%*

n = 640

nonresponse = 1

Are relations between employees and supervisors in your work unit characterized by conflict or cooperation? (all levels)

High levels of conflict	6.2%
Mostly conflict	16.3
Half and half	10.3
Mostly cooperation	30.2
High levels of cooperation	37.0
	100%

n = 796

nonresponse = 6

*Totals may vary from 100% owing to rounding error.

cations on bureaucratic capacity was examined by cross tabulating the various dimensions of bureaucratic capacity with the communication items appearing in Tables 4.4 and 4.5. The results did not support the hypothesis that open communications increased bureaucratic capacity.

Positive reinforcement was measured by two questionnaire items, the text and percentage distributions for which appear in Table 7.3. It will be noted from the data appearing in Table 7.3 that positive reinforcement is not a major feature of supervisory practice in the Egyptian bureaucracy. Only 15 percent of the respondents (middle and lower level) felt confident that their efforts were appreciated by their supervisors. Thirty-six percent did not know if their efforts were appreciated or not. The hypothesized link between positive reinforcement and productivity was difficult to ascertain due to the high percentage of "do not know" responses. Along the same lines, approximately one-third of the respondents reported tension between subordinates and supervisors. Low levels of positive reinforcement are also reflected in the low level of personal communication between supervisors and subordinates (Table 4.5).

Systemic Variables

Systemic variables represent one of the four major determinants of bureaucratic capacity. The Al Ahram questionnaire, accordingly, endeavored to ascertain the extent to which the behavioral dimensions of bureaucratic capacity were influenced by various systemic variables. Toward this end, the questionnaire contained several items relating to the adequacy of authority, information, and skills. As noted in chapter 2, the respondents were also asked to indicate the level of their outside employment. The questionnaire items and percentage distributions for the systemic items are presented in Table 7.4. By and large, they indicate little dissatisfaction with the systemic environment, the major exception being authority levels. Similar lack of concern with systemic variables, other than salary and incentives, was also manifest in the listing of the elements of job satisfaction and dissatisfaction presented in Table 3.4.

In terms of the influence of systemic variables upon bureaucratic behavior, it would seem logical to hypothesize that positive perceptions of systemic circumstances would result in enhanced behavioral performance. At the very least, enhanced environmental circumstances would appear to increase the mechanical prerequisites of productivity. Herzberg's theory of motivation discussed in chapter 3, however, would place systemic variables in the hygienic category, thereby suggesting that they should have little influence on professional behavior. Highly motivated individuals, in this view, work

Table 7.4

Systemic Influences on Bureaucratic Behavior
(n = 796)

Is your authority adequate to make the decisions your job requires you to make? (middle- and upper-level officials only)

Adequate	25.8
Usually adequate	39.5
Seldom adequate	20.8
Inadequate	13.9
	100%

nonresponse = 1

Do you possess adequate information and data to do your job properly? (all levels)

Adequate	67.3
Usually adequate	29.6
Seldom adequate	2.5
Inadequate	.6
	100%

nonresponse = 0

Do your job duties fit your education and training? (all levels)

Very well	71.6
Well enough	22.1
Poorly	6.3
	100%

nonresponse = 0

regardless of the systemic constraints. Poorly motivated individuals avoid work regardless of the opportunities.

The influence of systemic variables upon bureaucratic behavior was ascertained by cross tabulating the four systemic variables with the behavioral dimensions of bureaucratic capacity. The results, unfortunately, were inconclusive. Productivity was minimally influenced by either the adequacy of authority or the adequacy of information. On the other hand, officials willing to admit that their skills were inadequate to perform their assigned responsibilities were less productive as measured by the job-satisfaction indicator of productivity than officials who perceived their skills to be adequate ($g = .289$). It is also interesting to note that officials not having second jobs were more productive than those who did as measured by the professional-reference indicator of productivity ($g = .222$).

Also of some interest was the tendency of individuals upset with their systemic circumstances to be critical of bureaucratic attitudes toward the masses. The correlation between inadequate authority and a feeling that tension between the bureaucracy and the masses was the fault of the bureaucracy, for example, was ($g = .319$). The same tendency also occurred among individuals who felt that their skills were inadequate for their jobs.

Other Considerations

In addition to the variables reviewed above, productivity was also cross tabulated with recruitment and religion. These variables, however, proved to be unrelated to the various dimensions of behavioral capacity.

Summary and Conclusions

The chapter began with three basic questions: (1) which areas of the bureaucracy have the highest levels of behavioral capacity? (2) what factors are associated with high levels of behavioral capacity? and (3) how can behavioral capacity be strengthened? While a comprehensive examination of these questions must await the next chapter, the analysis of the present chapter suggested the following observations:

The High Performers

1. Productivity was concentrated in the upper levels of the bureaucracy. Middle-level officials were, by some measures, more productive than senior-level officials. The lowest level of the bureaucracy was clearly the least productive. Such distinctions, however, are not intended to suggest that any level of the bureaucracy was particularly productive.

2. Among upper-level officials, productivity was concentrated in the thirty-nine to fifty-five age group. Among middle- and lower-level officials, the age of productive officials was younger.

3. There was some suggestion that productive officials in the middle and lower levels of the bureaucracy were not being used effectively. There was certainly no indication that productive officials were more likely to receive foreign training than their less-productive peers.

4. Decision-making innovation was concentrated at the upper level of the bureaucracy.

5. Social innovation, flexibility, and mass regarding varied minimally when cross tabulated with the several independent variables. This finding suggests that attitudes toward social innovation, flexibility, and mass regarding are rooted deeply in Egyptian culture and may be very difficult to change.

The Attributes of High Performance

1. Education level was the dominant independent variable influencing productivity and decision-making innovation. Foreign and local training programs also appeared to influence productivity and innovation; however, the relationship disappeared when cross tabulations between the training and performance indicators were controlled for education level.

2. The most productive and innovative officials either preferred foreign media to the local media or established a balance between local and foreign media.

3. The environment of the Aluminum Corporation appeared to be more conducive to productivity and decision-making innovation than the environments of the Ministries of Industry and Social Affairs. The work environment of the Aluminum Corporation differed

from the work environment in the mainline ministries in four specific areas: (1) the group environment was more positive, (2) communication between supervisors and subordinates was more fluid (in spite of the strong desire of Aluminum Corporation officials to concentrate authority), (3) the morale of the Aluminum Corporation officials was bolstered by a feeling that they had been promoted promptly and that promotion procedures were fair, and (4) officials of the Aluminum Corporation were largely recruited from a rural environment and were not opposed to working in a rural environment.

8

✥

Summary, Conclusions, and Recommendations

The Al Ahram project was born of the realization that the Egyptian bureaucracy is probably the single most important actor in Egypt's drive for economic and social development. If the Egyptian bureaucracy cannot or will not play a decisive role in the developmental process, the economic and social development of Egypt will be slow and halting at best. What, then, the study asked, is the capacity of the Egyptian bureaucracy to play a dynamic role in the economic and social development of Egyptian society?

The assessment of Egypt's bureaucratic capacity addressed four basic dimensions of the bureaucratic process: bureaucratic structure, bureaucratic behavior, bureaucratic environment, and bureaucratic rapport with the public. Of these, particular emphasis was placed upon the behavioral dimension of bureaucratic capacity. This emphasis reflected the existence of excellent analyses of Egypt's bureaucratic structure and bureaucratic environment by Ayubi, Youssef, and others.

The methodologies of the Al Ahram study were many and varied. The analysis of bureaucratic structure, bureaucratic environment, and mass attitudes toward the bureaucracy relied heavily upon published works, Ph.D. dissertations, the Egyptian press, and informal interviews with a wide variety of scholars, government officials, and politicians. We would also be remiss if we did not acknowledge the prior research of Ali Leila and the participant observation of Ali Leila, El Sayed Yassin, and other members of the research team. The analysis of bureaucratic behavior was based upon the results of a sample survey administered to 826 Egyptian officials during the spring of 1983. The details of the survey are described in chapter 2.

The objectives of this final chapter are (1) to summarize the results of the survey, (2) to draw conclusions concerning the present bureaucratic capacity of the Egyptian bureaucracy, and (3) to recommend, within the limits of the data, strategies for increasing the developmental capacity of the Egyptian bureaucracy.

Summary of Results

The first objective of the Al Ahram project was to provide an empirical, baseline assessment of four dimensions of bureaucratic behavior requisite to the developmental capacity of the Egyptian bureaucracy: drive, flexibility, innovation, and mass regarding. It is doubtful that the empirical assessments provided by the Al Ahram study offer any surprises to students of Egyptian bureaucracy or Egyptian government. Indeed, the findings reinforced criticisms of the Egyptian bureaucracy that have long been prominent in the Egyptian press. The objective of assessing bureaucratic capacity, however, was not to provide surprises. It was to provide an empirical assessment of behavior that must be altered if the Egyptian bureaucracy is to play its essential role in the developmental process. Hunches not verified by empirical data make a poor basis for reform.

Drive and Productivity

Drive, as defined in terms of the Al Ahram project, involved two basic dimensions: productivity and motivation. The relevance of productivity and motivation to the developmental capacity are self-evident and do not require further elaboration at this point.

Assessing the productivity of bureaucratic officials is a subjective exercise at best. The most persuasive approach to the evaluation of bureaucratic productivity, in the view of the research team, was the job-satisfaction measure of productivity proposed and empirically tested by Herzberg, the details of which are described at some length in chapter 3. In addition to possessing empirical norms, the job-satisfaction measure is value-free and is easily applied in a variety of cross-national settings. As such, it was adopted as the primary measure of productivity employed by the Al Ahram study. The job-satisfaction measure of productivity was supplemented by two additional indicators of productivity: a professional-reference indicator and a work-value indicator. The supplemental measures of productivity did not have comparative norms.

Regardless of the measures used, Egyptian bureaucrats manifested productivity levels that were exceptionally low (Table 3.3). In terms of the job-satisfaction measure of productivity, for example, Egyptian norms were approximately 50 percentage points below corresponding norms for British civil servants. The supplemental measures of productivity also indicated low productivity levels. Regardless of how measured, then, the productivity level of Egyptian bureaucrats suggests that the Egyptian bureaucracy is unlikely to play a dynamic or even forceful role in the developmental process.

The second component of "drive" focused on the incentive values of Egyptian bureaucrats. In line with the work of Herzberg, the analysis suggested that monetary rewards alone were unlikely to stimulate more than marginal increases in productivity. Of the six incentive values examined (money, prestige, urban environment, security, ease, and proximity to relatives), prestige was by far and away the single most dominant incentive value manifested by the respondents. It was suggested, accordingly, that a prestige or status dimension be added to future incentive programs.

Flexibility

Bureaucratic flexibility is central to the developmental capacity of any bureaucracy. Flexibility enhances the ability of a bureaucracy to respond promptly and efficiently to the needs of the public. In so doing, it strengthens rapport between the masses and the government and enhances public confidence in and cooperation with the bureaucratic apparatus. Moreover, bureaucratic flexibility reduces waste by improving both the allocation of scarce resources and the coordination of bureaucratic efforts.

The analysis of bureaucratic flexibility focused upon two related processes: the willingness of senior officials to delegate authority and the corresponding willingness of subordinate officials to assume responsibility. On both counts, the respondents proved to be remarkably inflexible. Most senior officials did attempt to concentrate as much authority as possible in their own hands; most subordinates did

seek to avoid responsibility. While comparative norms for such behavior are not available, the magnitude of the percentages involved
suggests that the rigidity of the Egyptian bureaucracy severely re-
stricts its capacity to play a dominant role in the developmental
process.

Innovation

If Egypt is to provide a viable social and economic foundation
for future generations, it is essential that the bureaucracy provide new
and innovative solutions to the myriad economic and social problems
that are gradually pushing Egyptian society to the brink of despair.
The time-worn strategies of postponement and muddling through
simply are not working.

Lacking standard procedures or norms for assessing bureaucratic innovation, the Al Ahram study approached the topic from
two perspectives. First, senior officials were asked to assess the innovation levels of their subordinates. Second, respondents at all levels
were presented with a "decision-making innovation" index and a
"social-innovation index."

All of the measures of innovation indicated that innovation was
not the strong suit of the Egyptian bureaucracy. Few of the officials
surveyed manifested strong inclinations toward social innovation.

Mass Regarding

Most bureaucratic activity, directly or indirectly, involves interaction with the public. The more the public trusts, respects, and
cooperates with the bureaucracy, the easier it is for the bureaucracy to
accomplish its goals.

The Egyptian bureaucracy, as discussed at length in chapter 2,
has a long history of antagonism with the Egyptian public. The Al
Ahram study assessed the rapport problem from the perspective of
the bureaucracy. A survey of mass attitudes toward the bureaucracy,
while much needed, was beyond the scope of the project. As hypothesized, the data indicate the existence of a manifest gap in rapport
between the bureaucrats and their clients. This "rapport gap," from
the perspective of the bureaucrat, was based largely upon the inability

or unwillingness of the public to understand the role of bureaucrats and the constraints under which they work. An important ingredient in this "misunderstanding" was the pervasive desire of the masses to use *wasta* as a means of achieving their goals. In assessing the blame for the lack of rapport between the bureaucracy and the public, 75 percent of the respondents indicated that the fault lies with the public. This figure suggests that the bureaucracy is unlikely to take the first step in building greater rapport and greater cooperation between the two entities.

Explanations of Bureaucratic Behavior in Egypt

The second basic objective of the Al Ahram project was to examine the underlying roots of bureaucratic behavior in Egypt. Why is the Egyptian bureaucracy lethargic, inflexible, noninnovative, and lacking in rapport with the masses? An answer to this question must logically precede serious efforts at bureaucratic reform. It would also provide the basis for transferring bureaucratic technology within the Egyptian bureaucracy. It is far easier to build upon bureaucratic technology known to be effective in the Egyptian environment than it is to import technology geared to radically different political and social environments.

Efforts to examine the roots of bureaucratic behavior in Egypt included (1) scholarly analyses, press reports, and dissertations relating to the Egyptian bureaucracy, Egyptian government, Egyptian society, and Egyptian culture, (2) informal interviews with scholars and officials concerning the causes of Egypt's bureaucratic woes, (3) questionnaire items requesting senior respondents to evaluate the relevance of explanations of bureaucratic behavior offered by scholars and others, and (4) the analysis of the survey data.

Theoretical Explanations of Bureaucratic Behavior in Egypt

Explanations of bureaucratic behavior found in the secondary sources and interviews fell into five categories: systemic explanations, psychological explanations, cultural explanations, group dynamic explanations, and supervisor dynamic explanations. The systemic explanations focused on salaries, incentives, legal rigidities, recruitment policies, overstaffing, low skill levels, and other structural problems reviewed in chapters 1 and 2. The psychological explanations stressed the insecurity, alienation, and disinterest of Egyptian officials. Cultural explanations, in turn, stressed the authoritarian nature of the Egyptian family, the traditional emphasis on conformity rather than innovation, and the historically rooted antipathy between the rulers and the ruled. The group dynamic and supervisor dynamic explanations focused on the lack of interpersonal reinforcement for productive behavior within the bureaucracy.

The above explanations, it is interesting to note, varied markedly from source to source. The informal interviews with senior officials and the Egyptian press tended to stress the systemic explanations of bureaucratic behavior. Western social science theory emphasized psychological and cultural explanations. The recent public administration literature emphasized problems of supervisor dynamics and group dynamics.

Explanations of Egyptian Bureaucratic Behavior by Senior Officials

Understanding the manner in which senior officials explain the deficiencies of the bureaucracy is critical for at least two reasons. First, senior officials live with the problems of bureaucracy on a daily basis. They are far closer to the problem than outside observers. Second, senior officials will ultimately be the individuals charged with implementing bureaucratic reforms. They are far more likely to implement reforms that fit their perceptions than they are to address the abstract concepts of scholars. Quite clearly, explanations shared by both scholars and the senior officials are likely to have greater validity than explanations reflecting a single point of view.

The explanations of bureaucratic behavior offered by the senior officials were of interest on two counts. First, at least one-half of the senior officials surveyed acknowledged that all of the explanations of bureaucratic behavior suggested by the scholarly literature were important determinants of bureaucratic behavior in Egypt. This reinforces the view that the developmental problems confronting the Egyptian bureaucracy are complex and multifaceted. It also suggests that the problems confronting the bureaucracy are unlikely to be solved by a "quick fix" such as an across-the-board salary increase.

The second major point of interest was that the senior officials surveyed believed systemic factors to be the most important determinants of dysfunctional behavior among their employees in spite of their acknowledgment of the complexity of the behavioral process. In their view, substantial increases in skills and salaries would result in significant increases in bureaucratic capacity. It would seem clear from this attitude that systemic reforms are far more likely to receive the support of senior officials than reforms stressing factors such as group dynamics or supervisor dynamics. Particularly relevant to the latter point was the finding that the senior officials, themselves, manifested an extreme reluctance to delegate authority to their subordinates, a reluctance bolstered by the fear that their subordinates might misuse the authority thus delegated. The senior bureaucrats are clearly part of the problem.

Data-Based Explanations of Bureaucratic Behavior

The data analysis provided in chapter 7 was designed to (1) highlight those elements within the bureaucracy manifesting the highest levels of bureaucratic capacity, and (2) to provide an empirical test of the explanations of bureaucratic behavior reviewed above.

In terms of identifying the Egyptian bureaucracy's most productive elements, the analysis of chapter 7 suggested that senior- and middle-level officials were far more productive and far more innovative in their decision making than lower-level officials. The lower level of the bureaucracy is clearly the least productive area of a lethargic apparatus. Productivity and decision-making innovation increased with age, but only up to a point. The most productive individuals at the senior level of the bureaucracy were in the thirty-nine to fifty-five age group. Productive individuals in the middle and lower levels of the bureaucracy were substantially younger, suggesting that productive individuals lost interest in their work if their advancement was long delayed. The more productive and more innovative officials were also better educated than their peers, although education of itself was not a guarantee of productivity. Finally, it should be noted that the environment of the Aluminum Corporation proved to be more conducive to productivity and decision-making innovation than the environments of the Ministry of Industry or the Ministry of Social Affairs.

Of particular interest was the finding that only productivity and decision-making innovation displayed significant variation across job levels, job units, age, and education categories. The social innovation, flexibility, and mass regarding dimensions of bureaucratic capacity were both uniform and uniformly low throughout the bureaucracy. Further analysis of the productivity and decision-making items suggested that they represented dimensions of bureaucratic behavior that were relatively easy to acquire and reinforce via education and training inasmuch as they were less deeply rooted in Egyptian culture than the other behaviors under consideration. The resistance of Egyptian officials to social innovation and their inflexibility, by contrast, has deep roots within Egyptian culture. The low level of mass regarding, by the same token, represents a central element of Egyptian bureaucratic culture. It was suggested, accordingly, that it may be far easier to achieve increases in productivity and decision-making innovation than it will be to improve the flexibility of the bureaucracy or its relations with the masses. This conclusion was further reinforced by an analysis of the media habits of Egyptian bureaucrats, an analysis that found Egyptian officials to be locally oriented in their media consumption.

Testing Theoretical Explanations of Bureaucratic Behavior

The theoretical explanations of bureaucratic behavior, it will be recalled, fell into five categories: systemic explanations, psychological explanations, cultural/social explanations, group dynamic explanations, and supervisor dynamic explanations.

Systemic Explanations. Systemic variables influenced bureaucratic behavior in two specific areas. First, officials who perceived their job skills to be adequate tended to be more productive, flexible, and mass oriented than officials finding their skills to be inadequate. The link between job skill and productivity was also reflected in the link between education level and bureaucratic capacity reviewed above. Particularly interesting, however, was the minimal influence of training programs on the various dimensions of behavioral capacity when the influence of training programs was controlled for education.

Second, individuals holding second jobs were less productive than individuals not diluting their energies with secondary positions.

If salary levels do force officials to take secondary positions, and they do, then the low remuneration of Egyptian officials does depress productivity. It is difficult to see how the Egyptian government can enforce its prohibition against secondary positions until such time as it affords its officials an adequate wage. This finding does not contradict the analysis of wages and productivity presented in chapter 3, an analysis suggesting that wage levels are unlikely to increase productivity once they attain adequate levels. The current salary structure of the Egyptian bureaucracy is not adequate.

The remaining systemic dimensions assessed by the survey had minimal influence upon the behavioral dimensions of bureaucratic capacity. We would caution, however, that only a few systemic factors were included in the analysis. Also, the present analysis focused on the link between systemic factors and bureaucratic behavior and not upon the overall influence of systemic factors on the developmental capacity of the Egyptian bureaucracy. As indicated in chapters 1 and 2, the influence of systemic factors on the developmental capacity of the Egyptian bureaucracy is large, indeed.

Psychological Explanations. The psychological explanations of bureaucratic behavior stressed three themes: alienation, insecurity, and motivations. The evaluations of bureaucratic behavior made by the senior officials suggested that insecurity was a greater source of low behavioral capacity than alienation. The senior officials, themselves, also manifested considerable insecurity.

The peer evaluations suggested that Egyptian officials were more timid than lazy. They also suggested, however, that few officials would go out of their way to look for work. If not alienated, Egyptian officials are clearly passive.

The main psychological component of the Al Ahram study focused on incentive values. Individuals motivated by prestige and money were clearly more productive than individuals motivated by a desire for security, an urban environment, or an easy job. Prestige emerged as the dominant motivating factor among respondents at all levels.

Cultural Explanations. Cultural explanations of bureaucratic behavior suggested that the authoritarian and deference patterns which characterize Egyptian bureaucratic behavior represent a direct extension of the authoritarian and deference patterns found in the traditional Egyptian family.

While cultural influences were not examined by specific questionnaire items, most dimensions of the analysis indirectly reinforced the view that cultural variables were a major determinant of bureaucratic behavior. The point was manifest in the finding that productivity and decision-making innovation, the two dimensions of bureaucratic behavior most directly influenced by education and other external forces, were minimally tied to traditional cultural norms. Flexibility and social innovation, by contrast, tended to be culture bound and were minimally influenced by education and training.

Group Dynamic Explanations. Group dynamic and group cultural explanations suggest that group norms within the Egyptian bureaucracy mitigate against performance by stressing low productivity and by reinforcing bureaucratic solidarity in confronting the demands of both the government and the masses. Group norms were addressed by the group dynamic scale. Correlations between the group dynamics scale and the indicators of bureaucratic capacity were noteworthy on three counts. First, peer evaluations were generally positive, reinforcing the suggestion of a high level of solidarity within Egyptian bureaucratic culture. Second, variations in peer evaluations among age, sex, and job-level categories were virtually nil, a finding also suggesting the uniformity of Egyptian bureaucratic culture. Third, positive peer evaluations tended to be inversely correlated with innovative decision making, flexibility, and mass regarding. Innovative individuals and individuals inclined toward mass regarding, it would appear, are running against the group norm. Group norms, as measured by the group dynamic scale, were unrelated to productivity.

Supervisory Dynamic Explanations. The supervisory dynamic explanations of bureaucratic capacity focused on the interplay between superiors and subordinates. Particular concern was directed toward the openness of the supervisor-subordinate relationship and the level of positive reinforcement accorded subordinates by their superiors.

As discussed above, senior Egyptian officials do concentrate authority. They are reluctant to delegate authority, and they do manifest distrust of their subordinates. As might be expected given these circumstances, levels of informal interaction between superiors and subordinates were minimal. Indeed, the main topic of informal interaction between subordinates and superiors centered on gaining the intercession of superiors in dealing with governmental problems *(wasta)*. Such interaction patterns would appear more calculated to the strengthening of patron-client relationships than to the impartial rewarding of job performance.

In terms of positive reinforcement, the data indicate that approximately one-third of the lower- and middle-level respondents did not know if their supervisors spoke well of them.

Conclusions

1. The fundamental conclusion to be derived from the Al Ahram study is that the Egyptian bureaucracy lacks the developmental capacity to provide basic economic and social services for a population that is expected to double within two decades. The present level of essential services is minimally adequate. A further deterioration of the current level of services will have dire political, economic, and social consequences.

If Egypt is to survive the economic and social challenges of the coming decade, it must either strengthen the developmental capacity of its bureaucracy or provide incentives for the private sector to play a dominant role in the developmental process. The Egyptian bureaucracy's abdication of its developmental responsibilities would represent a dramatic break with Egypt's revolutionary goals and traditions. It would also force the Egyptian government to seek its salvation in uncharted waters. The results of the *infitah* remain obscure. Moreover, very little is known about the Egyptian private sector or the interaction of the public and private sectors.[1] In particular, it is not known if the private sector ranks higher in the various dimensions of developmental capacity than the public sector. Current debates concerning the developmental capacity of the private sector are largely emotional and ideological. Empirical research on the topic is essential.

2. A second fundamental conclusion of the Al Ahram study is that the deficiencies of the Egyptian bureaucracy find their roots in the broader configuration of Egyptian political and social life. Bureaucratic reform independent of environmental considerations will be of limited utility, a fact amply demonstrated by the reform efforts of the past three decades. Moreover, political leaders must not delude

themselves into believing that verbal attacks on the bureaucracy will compensate for their own confusion. Using the bureaucracy as a whipping boy does not constitute bureaucratic reform. Political leaders must provide the bureaucracy with goals that are clear, ordered in priority, and sustained over time. They must provide the political and financial support necessary for the achievement of those goals. And, above all, political leaders must decide if the bureaucracy is to be an instrument of development or an extension of the welfare system. They cannot have it both ways.

It must also be recognized that the behavior of Egyptian bureaucrats is largely an extension of Egyptian culture. The opening of the bureaucracy to the masses in the aftermath of the 1952 revolution and the welfare orientation of the revolutionary government broke the class orientation of the bureaucracy and infused it with the values of the middle and lower-middle classes. Moreover, the continuation of the graduates policy in the postrevolutionary era has ensured a steady infusion of popular culture into the bureaucracy. The more the various dimensions of bureaucratic capacity are grounded in popular Egyptian culture, the more difficult they will be to modify without a corresponding modification of Egyptian cultural norms in general.

Finally, the effectiveness of a bureaucracy is also conditioned by the trust and cooperation of its clients. It was the strong impression of the research team that mass attitudes toward the bureaucracy were passive if not openly hostile. This view has also found repeated expression in President Mubarak's appeals to the masses to place greater faith in the capacity of the Egyptian government to solve Egypt's social and economic problems. Urgent research is required to provide empirical data on mass attitudes toward the bureaucracy and the means by which those attitudes are best modified.

3. The third conclusion of the Al Ahram project is that structural changes in the bureaucracy, while a necessary element of bureaucratic reform, will be of minimal utility unless they are matched by concomitant changes in bureaucratic behavior. Improving formal channels of communication, for instance, will do little to improve the flexibility of the bureaucracy as long as senior officials are predisposed to concentrate authority in their own hands and subordinate officials are reluctant to assume responsibility. If senior bureaucrats want to consolidate their personal authority, they will do so in spite of the rules. The mere provision of the structural requisites of performance then does not guarantee that they will be put to productive ends. In

the words of a famous Egyptian proverb, you can lead a camel to water, but you can not make him drink.

The data similarly suggest that changes in the structure of the bureaucracy may be of limited utility in altering the behavior of Egyptian bureaucrats. It is not at all clear, for example, that across-the-board raises or similar quick fixes will result in marked improvements in production, innovation, flexibility, or mass regarding. Finally, we would caution that efforts to solve behavioral problems with structural solutions may end up creating new and unanticipated problems. Efforts to ease corruption by requiring multiple signatures, for example, may or may not reduce corruption. It will, however, exacerbate the complexity and rigidity of bureaucratic procedures and place further bureaucratic obstacles in the path of Egyptian citizens forced to deal with the bureaucracy at every juncture of their lives.

The above comments are not intended to minimize the importance of structural reforms. Structural reforms are urgent. They simply are not a panacea for Egypt's bureaucratic problems. To bill them as such would be to reduce their effectiveness by creating unrealistic expectations.

Recommendations

The "conclusions" of the Al Ahram study were general in nature and stressed the social and political context of bureaucratic reform. The recommendations of the present section, by contrast, focus on the empirical data provided by the Al Ahram survey and are capable of being implemented within the bureaucracy as presently constituted. We must reiterate that the objective of the Al Ahram study was to provide an overall assessment of the influence of bureaucratic behavior on the various dimensions of bureaucratic capacity. The results are indicative rather than conclusive. They are the starting point of the research required to ensure that future reforms of the Egyptian bureaucracy are based upon a sound empirical foundation. The recommendations, themselves, address seven areas of reform: wages and incentives, education and training, recruitment, job assignments, maximizing the use of high-performance individuals, the timing of bureaucratic reform, and the delineation of needed research.

Wages and Salaries

1. Wage and salary levels should be increased to the point at which they provide an adequate standard of living. This step is essential to attract and retain qualified individuals. It is also essential to reduce the negative influence of inadequate wages upon productivity and the other behavioral dimensions of bureaucratic capacity. The term *adequate wage* must be determined by additional research.

2. Once adequate salary levels have been achieved, additional increases in wages and salaries should be rigorously tied to performance. Performance-based incentives, in addition to rewarding productivity, may alter the complacency and welfare mentality so deeply ingrained within the culture of the Egyptian bureaucracy.

3. Strong emphasis should be placed upon prestige-based incentives. To the greatest extent possible, monetary incentives should be combined with highly visible symbols of prestige. In addition to emerging as the strongest motivational value of the respondents, prestige-based incentives have the added advantage of being compatible with and supported by the broader configuration of Egyptian cultural values.

Education and Training

1. The clear impact of education levels upon productivity and decision-making innovation suggests that bureaucratic reform begins at the university level, if not earlier.

2. The structure, content, and management of present training programs must be thoroughly reviewed. In particular, the content of training programs should include more than skills and procedures. Training programs must be revised to include materials on bureaucratic behavior and the importance of establishing rapport with the masses.

3. Selection of officials for advanced training programs and particularly foreign training programs must be tied to performance. Linking training to performance would help to ensure that the skills of the most productive individuals are being updated and extended. It would also serve as a tangible, prestige-based incentive for enhanced performance.

Recruitment

Bureaucratic recruitment should stress quality. The continued welfare, dumping-ground basis of recruitment can only guarantee the continued lethargy of the bureaucracy.

Job Assignments

1. To the greatest extent possible, individuals should be placed in the areas of their competence.

2. All efforts should be made to place individuals in the geographic area of their preference. The burdens of commuting in the Cairo metroplex produce stress and fatigue. Transportation problems, it might be noted, were the number one source of job dissatisfaction among female employees.

Geographical considerations are particularly relevant to the critical efforts of the Egyptian government to alleviate the concentration of bureaucratic personnel in Cairo. Officials that have long been residents of Cairo are likely to resist transfer to provincial centers. Forced relocations would further depress bureaucratic morale and might reduce productivity. The data from the Aluminum Corporation, by contrast, indicate that individuals from the provinces have little objection to working in the provinces. It would seem, accordingly, that bureaucratic morale and perhaps bureaucratic capacity could be enhanced by staffing decentralized units with individuals from the region in which they are located.

Maximizing the Use of Productive Individuals

1. Better means must be devised to identify those individuals in the bureaucracy ranking high in productivity, flexibility, innovation, and mass regarding. This could be accomplished by supplementing supervisory evaluations with an externally administered instrument (written or oral) designed to identify individuals likely to rank high in the various areas of bureaucratic capacity. Questionnaire items used in the Al Ahram survey suggest the feasibility of such an instrument. The work-value scale, the innovation items, and the productivity

indicators would appear to be particularly relevant to this undertaking. Such an instrument should be grounded in Egyptian culture and practice and, as such, should be constructed by Egyptian social scientists rather than borrowed directly from abroad. Related instruments could also be used for recruitment and placement purposes.

2. The most productive individuals must receive differential monetary and symbolic rewards. Providing high-performance officials with differential rewards will increase their utility as role models for officials in the formative stages of development. It should also strengthen their resolve to withstand the negative pressures of the work group.

3. All efforts must be made to place individuals scoring high on the various performance indicators in job situations which maximize their skills and talents. High performers are simply too valuable to waste.

4. Individuals ranking high on the performance indicators should receive preferential placement in foreign training programs. Such preferential selections will serve three objectives. First, it will provide training to individuals most likely to benefit from the training. Second, it will serve as prestige-based recognition and reinforcement for the productive individuals. Third, it will enhance the visibility of the productive individuals and enhance their capacity to serve as role models for younger officials.

5. A "fast-track" training and promotion program should be implemented for students and junior bureaucrats ranking high on the various performance indicators.

The Timing of Bureaucratic Reform

1. Bureaucratic reform should initially focus on areas in which senior officials recognize and support the need for reform. In this regard, senior officials are most aware of the need for incentives that discriminate among employees and the need to improve both the development and allocation of skills. It is important that greater flexibility in the allocation of incentives be monitored to minimize its high potential for abuse.

2. Bureaucratic reform should initially stress productivity and decision-making innovation, the two areas of performance suggested by the data as being the most amenable to modification.

Additional Research

It is essential that future reforms of the Egyptian bureaucracy be grounded on a solid foundation of empirical research. Emotions and slogans are no longer enough. The Al Ahram project was conceived as one step in this process. It was designed to provide a general assessment of the behavioral problems confronting the bureaucracy and to provide a backdrop for more detailed research in specific problem areas. As such, the Al Ahram project pointed to the need for urgent research in the following areas:

1. Cross-unit comparisons. Differences in productivity between the Aluminum Corporation and the mainline ministries suggest that a high potential for the internal transfer of technology does exist within the Egyptian bureaucracy. To be fully exploited, this potential must be extended by research designed to identify the most productive work units within the bureaucracy and to better understand why the high-performance units are more productive than their less-productive counterparts. The latter objective is best achieved by comparing high- and low-performance units on all dimensions of the bureaucratic process including structure, behavior, and interaction with their political, economic, and social environments. The units of analysis should be small and amenable to a variety of research techniques including case studies and participant observation.

2. Motivational Values. The results of the work-value scale were among the most important of the Al Ahram project. As motivation is the key to productivity, additional research in this area is clearly essential.

3. Mass Rapport. The poor rapport between the bureaucracy and the mass is a major obstacle to trust and cooperation between the two entities. The Al Ahram project addressed the problem from the perspective of the bureaucracy. Corresponding data analyzing mass attitudes toward the bureaucracy and the government are essential to improving one of the weakest areas of bureaucratic capacity in Egypt.

4. Interface between the Public and Private Sector. The developmental capacity of the private sector is largely a matter of conjecture and ideology. Assessments of the role that the private sector is capable of playing in the development process must be based upon empirical data. Empirical studies must also address the most effective means of facilitating the interface between the public and private sectors.

5. Identifying High-performance Individuals. One of the easiest, least costly, and most important steps toward bureaucratic reform in Egypt would be the design, testing, and implementation of a screening instrument designed to *assist* in the identification of potentially productive officials and applicants.

Notes

1—Bureaucracy in Egypt: An Overview

1. We are indebted to Hassan Youssef Pasha, former head of the Royal Diwan, for his many insights into the bureaucratic process during the final years of the monarchy. The views expressed herein are those of the authors and not those of Mr. Hassan Youssef. Particularly insightful are Hassan Youssef's memoirs: *The Palace: Its Role in Egyptian Politics, 1922–1952* (Cairo: Al Ahram, 1982. Arabic text). For an interesting view of this period one might also consult Jacques Berque, *Egypt: Imperialism and Revolution* (New York: Praeger, 1972).

2. John Waterbury, *The Egypt of Nasser and Sadat: The Political Economy of Two Regimes* (Princeton, N.J.: Princeton University Press, 1983); R. Hrair Dekmejian, *Egypt Under Nasser* (Albany, N.Y.: State University of New York Press, 1971); Derek Hopwood, *Egypt: Politics and Society 1945–1981* (London: Allen and Unwin, 1982); P. J. Vatikiotis, *Nasser and His Generation* (New York: St. Martin's Press, 1979).

3. *Arab Political Encyclopedia,* (Cairo: Documentation and Research Center, Information Department, July 1961) pp. 42–49.

4. Abdel-Karim Ibrahim Darwish, "Bureaucracy and Social Change in Modern Egypt" (Ph.D. dissertation, New York University, 1962).

5. John S. Badeau, "The Problem of Stability Among Middle East Governments" in Harvey P. Hall, ed., *The Evolution of Public Responsibility in the Middle East* (Washington, D.C.: The Middle East Institute, 1955).

6. Nazih N. M. Ayubi, "Bureaucratic Inflation and Administrative Inefficiency: The Deadlock in Egyptian Administration," *Middle East Studies* 18, no. 3 (July 1982), pp. 286–99.

7. Frederick Harbison and Ibrahim Abdelkader Ibrahim, *Human Resources for Egyptian Enterprise* (New York: McGraw-Hill, 1958).

8. Samir M. Youssef, *System of Management in Egyptian Public Enterprises* (Cairo: Center for Middle East Management Studies, The American University in Cairo, 1983) pp. 26–27.

9. Darwish, "Bureaucracy and Social Change," chapters 7 and 8.

10. Ramzi Zaki, *The Egyptian Economic Crisis* (Cairo: Library Madbouli, 1983. Arabic text). Chapter 9 is particularly relevant to this topic. Also see: Henry J. Burton,

Four Issues on Economic Policy in Egypt (Cairo: Ministry of Economy, Foreign Trade and Economic Cooperation, 1980); Economic Studies Unit, *Recent Developments in Egyptian Economy* (Cairo: Ministry of Economy, Foreign Trade and Economic Cooperation, 1981); Henry J. Burton, "Egypt's Development in the Seventies," *Economic Development and Cultural Change* 31, no. 4 (1983) pp. 679–904; Kate Gillespie, *Tripartite Relationship: Government, Foreign Investors, and Local Investors During Egypt's Economic Opening* (New York: Praeger, 1984).

11. This discussion is based upon interviews conducted in Cairo during the period 1982–86. Extensive treatment of the United States aid program in Cairo is also to be found in: William J. Burns, *Economic Aid and American Policy Toward Egypt, 1955–1981* (Albany, N.Y.: State University of New York Press, 1984); Marvin G. Weinbaum, *Egypt and the Politics of U.S. Economic Aid* (Boulder, Colo.: Westview Press, 1986).

12. Allen Kopec, "USAID In Egypt: An Interview with Frank Kimball, Director of USAID in Egypt," *Cairo Today,* November 1985, pp. 16–17.

13. Ayubi, "Bureaucratic Inflation and Administrative Inefficiency." In this article Ayubi notes that between 1952 and the end of the 1960s, Egypt produced some 250,000 university graduates, all of whom found employment in the bureaucracy.

14. Zaki, *The Egyptian Economic Crisis,* p. 109.

15. *Al Ahram* (Cairo Arabic Daily), May 3, 1977.

16. *Rose Al Yousif* (Cairo Arabic Weekly), February 13, 1978.

17. *Al Ahrar* (Cairo Arabic Daily), December 16, 1977.

18. *Al Ahram,* July 8, 1977.

19. President Hosni Mubarak, "Presentation before the Economic Conference: February 13, 1982," *Speeches and Discussions of President Hosni Mubarak: January 1982–July 1982* (Cairo: Ministry of Information, January 1983.) pp. 66–67.

20. Ibid.

21. Zaki, *The Egyptian Economic Crisis,* chapter 9.

22. Gregory Kats, "The Population Factor," *Cairo Today,* January 1983, pp. 26–44.

23. Mamduh Mahran, "In the Control Center: An Investigation," *Al Mussawar* (Cairo Arabic Weekly), June 8, 1984.

24. Mubarak, "Presentation before the Economic Conference."

25. President Hosni Mubarak, "Speech Opening the New Session of the Egyptian Parliament: November 13, 1985," *Al Ahram,* November 14, 1985.

26. Ibid.

27. Ibid.

28. Irving Louis Horowitz, "The 'Rashomon' Effect: Ideological Proclivities and Political Dilemmas of the IMF," *Journal of Interamerican Studies,* 27, no. 4 (Winter 1985–86).

29. "Hosni Mubarak: This is my word to the Arab Summit in Amman," *Al Watan Al Arabi,* no. 34-560, November 6, 1987, pp. 28–33.

2—The Bureaucratic Milieu

1. For an excellent review of material on this topic see: Ferrel Heady, *Public Administration: A Comparative Perspective,* 2nd ed. (New York: Marcel Dekker, 1979).

Earlier works include Fred W. Riggs, ed., *Frontiers of Development Administration* (Durham, N.C.: Duke University Press, 1970); Raalph Braibanti, ed., *Political and Administrative Development* (Durham, N.C.: Duke University Press, 1969); Joseph LaPalombara, ed., *Bureaucracy and Political Development* (Princeton, N.J.: Princeton University Press, 1963); John D. Montgomery and William Siffin, eds., *Approaches to Development: Politics, Administration and Change* (New York: McGraw Hill, 1966); Lee Sigelman, "In Search of Comparative Administration," *Public Administration Review* 36, no. 6, (1976), pp. 621–25; Dwight Waldo, *Comparative Public Administration: Prologue, Problems, and Promise* (Chicago: Comparative Public Administration Group, American Society for Public Administration, 1964); Jong Jun, "Renewing the Study of Comparative Administration: Some Reflections on the Current Possibilities," *Public Administration Review* 36, no. 6 (1976), pp. 641–47; Krishna K. Tummala, ed., *Administrative Systems Abroad* Revised edition, (Lanham, Maryland: University Press of America, Inc., 1984).

2. Abdel-Karim Ibrahim Darwish, "Bureaucracy and Social Change in Modern Egypt" (Ph.D. dissertation, New York University, 1962).

3. Richard F. Nyrop, ed., *Egypt: A Country Study* (Washington, D.C.: Foreign Area Studies, The American University, 1983) p. 198.

4. Ibid.

5. President Hosni Mubarak, "Address to the Egyptian Parliament: November 13, 1985," *Al Ahram,* November 14, 1985.

6. Nazih N. M. Ayubi, *Bureaucracy and Politics in Contemporary Egypt* (London: Ithaca Press, 1980); Samir M. Youssef, *System of Management in Egyptian Public Enterprises* (Cairo: Center for Middle East Management Studies, The American University, 1983).

7. Ramzi Zaki, *The Egyptian Economic Crisis* (Cairo: Library Madbouli, 1983) p. 78.

8. Ayubi, *Bureaucracy and Politics in Contemporary Egypt,* pp. 295–96.

9. Zaki, *The Egyptian Economic Crisis,* chapter 3.

10. Zaki, *The Egyptian Economic Crisis,* p. 31.

11. Zaki, *The Egyptian Economic Crisis,* chapter 5.

12. Youssef, *System of Management,* p. 127.

13. Youssef, *System of Management,* chapter 4.

14. E. W. Lane, *Manners and Customs of the Modern Egyptians* (London: J. M. Dent & Sons, Ltd., 1908).

15. Problems of corruption, favoritism, nepotism, and so forth, are discussed openly in the Egyptian press and particularly in the opposition papers. See, for example, *Al Shab,* July 20, 1980, or September 30, 1980.

16. See note 1 for a listing of some representative works.

17. Frederick Herzberg, *The Managerial Choice* (Homewood, Ill.: Dow Jones-Irwin, 1976). See chapter 2.

18. President Hosni Mubarak, "Speech Opening the New Session of the Egyptian Parliament: November 13, 1985," *Al Ahram,* November 14, 1985.

19. This view is based upon extensive research by Dr. Ali Leila of Ein Shams University in Cairo.

20. *The Egyptian Gazette,* March 24, 1982.

21. Morroe Berger, *Bureaucracy and Society in Modern Egypt* (Princeton, N.J.: Princeton University Press, 1957); Ayubi, *Bureaucracy and Politics in Contemporary Egypt.*

22. Ayubi, "Bureaucratic Inflation and Administrative Efficiency: The Deadlock in Egyptian Administration," *Middle East Studies* 18, no. 3 (July 1982) p. 293.

23. Ibid. p. 287.

24. Youssef, *System of Management,* chapter 1.

25. Saad Eddin-Din Ibrahim, *Toward a Sociological Theory for Development in the Third World* (Second Annual Scientific Conference for Egyptian Economists, Cairo, March 1977. Arabic text).

26. Youssef, *System of Management,* p. 127.

27. An extensive discussion of the special problems of conducting survey research in the Middle East can be found in Mark Tessler, Monte Palmer, Tawfic Farfah, and Barbara Ibrahim, *The Evaluation and Application of Survey Research in the Arab World* (Bolder, Colo.: Westview, 1987).

28. Youssef; Berger; Ayubi, *Bureaucracy and Politics in Contemporary Egypt;* Farid A. Muna, *The Arab Executive* (London: Macmillan, 1981).

3—Apathy, Values, Incentives, and Development

1. Henry J. Burton, *Four Issues on Economic Policy in Egypt* (Cairo: Ministry of Economy, Foreign Trade and Economic Cooperation, 1980); Economic Studies Unit, *Recent Developments in Egyptian Economy* (Cairo: Ministry of Economy, Foreign Trade and Economic Cooperation, 1981); Henry J. Burton, "Egypt's Development in the Seventies" *Economic Development and Cultural Change* 31, no. 4 (1983), pp. 679–704. Also see Marvin G. Weinbaum and Rasid Naim, "Domestic and International Politics in Egypt's Economic Policy Reforms" (Paper presented at the convention of the Middle East Studies Association of North America, Chicago, November 1983).

2. Abdul As Satar Al Taweil, "Self Development: Easy and Difficult, *Rose Al Youssef* (Arabic language weekly) February 4, 1985, p. 26.

3. Patricia W. Ingraham and Charles Barrilleau, "Motivating Government Managers for Retrenchment: Some Possible Lessons from the Senior Executive Service" *Public Administration Review* 43, no. 5 (1983), pp. 393–402.

4. Nazih N. M. Ayubi, "Bureaucratic Inflation and Administrative Inefficiency: The Deadlock in Egyptian Administration," *Middle Eastern Studies,* 18, no. 3 (1982), pp. 286–99.

5. An excellent review of various incentive formats is provided in: Gary A. Yukl, *Leadership in Organizations* (Englewood Cliffs, N.J.: Prentice Hall, 1981). Chapters 6 and 7 are particularly relevant.

6. The professional-reference indicators were based on responses to the following item:

What sources of information do you find most useful for your job?

The responses were

radio	6.7
television	14.4
papers	13.5
professional materials	34.1
associations	1.4

friends	1.6
relatives	.1
colleagues	5.9
boss	18.1
other	4.2
	100%

7. Highly productive individuals on the work-value indicator of productivity were those individuals who did not pick comfort or security over any of the other competing incentive values appearing in Table 3.7, or who picked either comfort or security to be dominant only once over one of the competing incentive values appearing in Table 3.7. The least productive category was created by combining individuals who ranked comfort as the superior value in Table 3.7 at least twice with individuals who ranked security as the superior value at least twice. Individuals falling between the two extremes constituted the middle category.

8. Our division of responses into high productivity and low productivity and low-productivity choices was based upon the judgment of the research team and reflects related categorizations by Herzberg and others. See: Frederick Herzberg, *The Managerial Choice* (Homewood, Ill.: Dow Jones-Irwin, 1976), chapter 2.

9. See explanatory note on Table 3.2.

10. Hugh Livingstone and Roy Wilkie, "Motivation and Performance Among Civil Service Managers," *Public Administration* 59, no. 5 (Summer 1981), pp. 151–73.

11. The Gamma is an ordinal-level error reduction statistic. A Gamma of .200 between education level and professionalism, by way of illustration, could be interpreted to mean that knowledge that a group has a high level of education would increase the probability of that group being more professional than comparison groups by approximately 20 percent.

12. Unless otherwise indicated, all coefficients are significant at .05 level or better.

13. Morroe Berger, *Bureaucracy and Society in Egypt* (Princeton, N.J.: Princeton University Press, 1957); Nazih N. M. Ayubi, *Bureaucracy and Politics in Contemporary Egypt* (London: Ithaca Press, 1980); Farid A. Muna, *The Arab Executive* (London: MacMillan, 1981).

14. Eddin C. Nevis, "Using an American Perspective in Understanding Another Culture: Toward a Hierarchy of Needs for the People's Republic of China," *Journal of Applied Behavioral Science* 19, no. 4 (1981).

15. Efiong J. Etuk, "Middle Managers in Cross River State of Nigeria Public Service," *Indian Journal of Public Administration* 27, no. 4 (1981), pp. 994–1005.

16. Mason Haire, Edwin E. Ghiselli, and Lyman W. Porter, *Managerial Thinking* (New York: John Wiley, 1966).

17. Ingraham and Barrilleau, "Motivating Government Managers," p. 397.

18. Livingstone and Wilkie, "Motivation and Performance," p. 165.

19. Richard Chackerian and Suliman Shadukhi, "Public Bureaucracy in Saudi Arabia," *International Review of Administrative Sciences* XLIX, no. 3 (1983), pp. 319–22.

4—Bureaucratic Flexibility and Development in Egypt

1. H. A. Attrabi, *Egypt: Problems and Solutions* (in Arabic) (Cairo: Library Madbouli, 1982); Nazih N. M. Ayubi, *Bureaucracy and Politics in Contemporary Egypt* (London: Ithaca Press, 1980); Nazih N. M. Ayubi, "Bureaucratic Inflation and Administrative Efficiency: The Deadlock in Egyptian Administration," *Middle Eastern Studies* 18, no. 3 (1982); Morroe Berger, *Bureaucracy and Society in Egypt* (Princeton, N.J.: Princeton University Press, 1957); Farid A. Muna, *The Arab Executive* (London: Macmillan, 1981); J. Waterbury, *Egypt, Burdens of the Past: Options for the Future* (Bloomington, Ind.: Indiana University Press, 1978).

2. Mamdouh Mahran, "In the Control Room" (in Arabic) *Al Mussawar,* June 8, 1984.

3. Samir M. Youssef, *System of Management in Egyptian Public Enterprises* (Cairo: Center for Middle East Management Studies, the American University of Cairo, 1983).

4. Ibid.

5. M. Haire, E. E. Ghiselli, and L. W. Porter, *Managerial Thinking: An International Study* (New York: Wiley, 1966); Frederick Herzberg, *The Managerial Choice* (Homewood, Ill.: Dow Jones-Irwin, 1976); G. A. Yukl, *Leadership in Organizations* (Englewood Cliffs, N.J.: Prentice Hall, 1981).

5—Innovation and Bureaucracy in Egypt

1. Mavis Puthucheavy, *The Politics of Administration: The Malaysian Experience* (London: Oxford University Press, 1978); Monte Palmer et al., "Bureaucratic Innovation and Economic Development in the Middle East: A Study of Egypt, Saudi Arabia and the Sudan" (forthcoming).

2. Victor A. Thompson, *Bureaucracy and Innovation* (Tuscaloosa, Ala.: University of Alabama Press, 1969).

3. Alex Inkeles and David H. Smith, *Becoming Modern* (Cambridge, Mass.: Harvard University Press, 1974). See chapters 2 and 18.

4. Nazih N. M. Ayubi, *Bureaucracy and Politics in Contemporary Egypt* (London: Ithaca Press, 1980); Samir M. Youssef, *System of Management in Egyptian Public Enterprises* (Cairo: Center for Middle East Management Studies, The American University, 1983) pp. 26–7.

5. Frederick Herzberg, *The Managerial Choice* (Homewood, Ill.: Dow Jones-Irwin, 1976). See chapter 2.

6. Sania Hamady, *Temperament and Character of the Arabs* (New York: Twayne Publishers, 1960).

7. Ernest Gellner, "The Tribal Society and its Enemies," in Richard Tapper, ed., *The Conflict of Tribe and State,* (London: Croom Helm, 1983); Ernest Gellner, *Muslim Society* (London: Cambridge University Press, 1981).

8. D. C. McClelland, *The Achieving Society* (Princeton, N.J.: Van Nostrand, 1961).

9. Morroe Berger, *Bureaucracy and Society in Egypt* (Princeton, N.J.: Princeton University Press, 1957).

10. Nazih N. M. Ayubi, "Bureaucracies: Expanding Size, Changing Roles" (Paper presented before the International Conference on State, Nation and Integration in the Arab World, Corfu, 1–6 September 1984).

6—Bureaucracy and the Public

1. President Hosni Mubarak, "Address to the Egyptian Parliament," November 13, 1985, *Al Ahram,* November 14, 1985.

2. Ali Lutfi, "Ten Economic Causes," (Cairo: *Al Ahram Iktisadi,* no. 869 (September 9, 1985), p. 10 (translated by M. Palmer).

3. *Al Ahram,* May 6, 1977.

4. This and other questionnaire items preceded with an asterisk in the tables were presented in inverse order as part of a procedure designed to test for response bias.

5. Mubarak, "Address to the Egyptian Parliament," November 13, 1985.

6. Ibid.

7. Stanford W. Gregory, Jr., "Auto Traffic in Egypt as a Verdant Grammar," *Social Psychology Quarterly* 48, no. 4 (1985), pp. 337–48.

7—The Attributes of Bureaucratic Performance

1. The Gamma is an ordinal-level error reduction statistic. See chapter 3, note 11.

2. Frederick Herzberg, *The Managerial Choice* (Homewood, Ill.: Dow Jones-Irwin, 1976).

3. Individuals indicating that they did not have occasion to interact with the public have been deleted from the analysis of mass regarding.

4. See page 36 of chapter 2.

5. Coefficients are not provided for nominal-level data.

6. Earl L. Sullivan, *Women in Egyptian Public Life* (Syracuse, N.Y.: Syracuse University Press, 1986); Bent Hansen and Samir Radwan, *Employment Opportunities and Equity in Egypt* (Geneva: International Labor Office, 1982).

7. In addition to the discussion of sex and work values presented in chapter 3, data relating to sex and religious differences in the social and cultural behavior of the respondents in the Al Ahram project will be published shortly by *Cairo Papers.* The exact title has yet to be determined.

8. Daniel Lerner, *The Passing of Traditional Societies* (Glencoe, Ill.: Free Press, 1958).

9. Max Weber, *The Theory of Social and Economic Organization* (New York: Macmillan, 1947).

10. Paul Hersey and Ken Blanchard, *Management of Organizational Behavior,* fourth ed. (Englewood Cliffs, N.J.: Prentice Hall, 1982).

11. Perry M. Smith, *Taking Charge* (Washington, D.C.: National Defense University Press, 1986).

8—Summary, Conclusions, and Recommendations

1. John Waterbury, professor of political science at Princeton University, is currently conducting research on the interface between the public and private sectors.

Bibliography

Abdel-Khalek, G., and Tignor, R. 1982. *The Political Economy of Income Distribution in Egypt.* New York: Holmes and Meier.

Addo, N. (ed.). 1985. *Development as Social Transformation.* Boulder, Colo.: Westview Press.

Adedeji, A., and Shaw, T. M. (eds.). 1985. *Economic Crisis in Africa: African Perspectives on Development Problems and Potentials.* Boulder, Colo.: Lynne Rienner Publishers, Inc.

Anker, R. and Hein, C. 1986. *Sex Inequalities in Urban Employment: The Third World.* New York: St. Martin's.

Astley, W. G. and Va de Ven, H. A. 1983. Central perspectives and debates in organization theory. *Administrative Science Quarterly 28(2),* 245–73.

Attir, M. O., et al. (eds.). 1981. *Directions of Change: Modernization Theory, Research and Realities.* Boulder, Colo.: Westview Press.

Attrabi, H. A. 1982. *Egypt: Problems and Solutions* (in Arabic). Cairo: Library Madbouli.

Ayubi, N. M. 1980. *Bureaucracy and Politics in Contemporary Egypt.* London: Ithaca Press.

Ayubi, N. M. 1982. Bureaucratic inflation and administrative inefficiency: The deadlock in Egyptian administration. *Middle Eastern Studies 18(3),* 286–99.

Ayubi, N. M. 1984. Bureaucracies: Expanding size, changing roles. Paper presented before the International Conference on State, Nation and Integration in the Arab World. Corfu, September 1–6.

Badeau, J. S. 1955. The problem of stability among Middle East governments. In Hall, H. P. (ed.), *The Evolution of Public Responsibility in the Middle East.* Washington, D.C.: The Middle East Institute.

Barrow, J. C. 1977. The variables of leadership: A review and conceptual framework. *Academy of Management Review 2(2),* 231–51.

Bartelmus, P. 1986. *Environment and Development.* London: Allen and Unwin.

Beer, M. 1980. *Organizational Change and Development: A Systems View.* Glenview, Ill.: Scott Foresman.

Berg, R. J., and Whitaker, J. S. (eds.). 1986. *Strategies for African Development*. Berkeley: University of California Press.

Berger, M. 1957. *Bureaucracy and Society in Modern Egypt*. Princeton: Princeton University Press.

Berque, J. 1972. *Egypt: Imperialism and Revolution*. New York: Praeger.

Binder, L., Coleman, J. S., La Palombara, J., Pye, L. W., Verba, S., and Weiner, M. 1971. *Crises and Sequences on Political Development*. Princeton: Princeton University Press.

Birks, J. S., and Sinclair, C. A. 1980. *Arab Manpower*. New York: St. Martin's Press.

Blair, H. W. 1981. *The Political Economy of Participation in Local Development Programs*. Ithaca, N.Y.: Cornell University, Center for International Studies.

Blair, H. W. 1985. Reorienting development administration. *The Journal of Development Studies 21(3)*, 449–57.

Bolman, L., and Deal, T. 1984. *Modern Approaches to Understanding and Managing Organizations*. San Francisco: Jossey-Bass.

Bowden, P. 1986. Problems of implementation. *Public Administration and Development 6(1)*, 61–71.

Braibanti, R. (ed.). 1969. *Political and Administrative Development*. Durham, N.C.: Duke University Press.

Brinkerhoff, D., and Ingle, M. 1987. *Integrating Blueprint and Process: A Structured Flexibility Approach to Development Management*. College Park, Md.: International Development Management Center, University of Maryland.

Bryant, C., and White, L. G. 1982. *Managing Development in the Third World*. Boulder: Westview Press.

Burns, W. J. 1984. *Economic Aid and American Policy Toward Egypt, 1955–1981*. Albany, N.Y.: State University of New York Press.

Burton, H. J. 1983. Egypt's development in the seventies. *Economic Development and Cultural Change, 31(4)*.

Burton, H. J. 1980. *Four Issues on Economic Policy in Egypt*. Cairo: Ministry of Economy, Foreign Trade and Economic Cooperation.

Burton, H. J. 1981. *Recent Developments in Egyptian Economy*. Cairo: Ministry of Economy, Foreign Trade and Economic Cooperation.

Caiden, N., and Wildavsky, A. 1974. *Planning and Budgeting in Poor Countries*. New York: Wiley.

Cantori, L. J., and Harik, I. H. (eds.). 1984. *Local Politics and Development in the Middle East*. Boulder: Westview Press.

Cates, C. 1979. Beyond muddling: Creativity. *Public Administration Review 39(6)*, 527–32.

Chackerian, R., and Shadukhi, S. 1983. Public bureaucracy in Saudi Arabia. *International Review of Administrative Sciences, XLIX(3)*, 319–22.

Chase, G., and Reveal, E. 1983. *How to Manage the Public Sector*. New York: Addison Wesley.

Clark, P., and Wilson, J. Q. 1961. Incentive systems. *Administrative Science Quarterly 6(1),* 129–66.

Cleaves, P. S. 1980. Implementation amidst scarcity and apathy: Political power and policy design. In Crindle, M. (ed.), *Politics and Policy Implementation in the Third World,* 281–303. Princeton: Princeton University Press.

Cohen, J., Grindle, M., and Walker, S. 1985. Foreign aid and conditions precedent: Political and bureaucratic dimensions. *World Development 13(12),* 1211–30.

Crozier, M., and Thoenig, J. C. 1976. The regulation of complex organized systems. *Administrative Science Quarterly 21(4),* 547–70.

Cunningham, J. B. 1977. Approaches to the evaluation of organizational effectiveness. *Academy of Management Review 2(3),* 463–74.

Danielson, M. N., and Keles, R. 1985. *The Politics of Rapid Urbanization.* New York: Holmes and Meier.

Darwish, A. I. 1962. Bureaucracy and Social Change in Modern Egypt. Ph.D. dissertation, New York University.

Davis, T. R., and Luthans, F. A. 1980. A social learning approach to organizational behavior. *Academy of Management Review 5(2),* 281–90.

Dekmejian, R. H. 1971. *Egypt Under Nasser.* Albany, N.Y.: State University of New York Press.

Delacrois, J., and Ragin, C. 1978. Modernizing institutions, mobilization, and Third World development: A cross-national study. *American Journal of Sociology 84,* 123–50.

Denhardt, R. B. 1984. *Theories of Public Organization.* Monterey, Calif.: Brooks/Cole.

Deva, S. 1979. Western conceptualization of administrative development. *International Review of Administrative Sciences 45(1),* 59–63.

Downs, A., and Mohr, L. 1979. Towards a theory of innovation. *Administration and Society 10,* 379–408.

Dzakpasu, C. K. 1978. Modern management techniques in public enterprise and training in Africa. *African Administrative Studies 19(July),* 65–70.

Economic Studies Unit, 1981. *Recent Developments in Egyptian Economy.* Cairo: Ministry of Economy, Foreign Trade and Economic Cooperation.

Elkin, S. L. 1983. Towards a contextual theory of innovation. *Policy Sciences 15(3),* 367–87.

Esman, M. J. 1978. Development administration and constituency organization. *Public Administration Review 38(2),* 166–72.

Esman, M. J. 1980. Development assistance in public administration: Requiem or renewal. *Public Administration Review 40(5),* 426–31.

Etuk, E. J. 1981. Middle managers in Cross River State of Nigeria Public Service. *Indian Journal of Public Administration 27(4),* 994–1005.

Fidler, L. A., and Johnson, J. D. 1984. Communication and innovation implementation. *Academy of Management Review 9(4),* 704–11.

Fiol, F. M., and Lyles, M. A. 1985. Organizational learning. *Academy of Management Review 10(4)*, 803–13.

Fransman, M. 1985. Conceptualizing technical change in the Third World in the 1980s. *Journal of Development Studies, 21(4)*, 572–653.

Garcia-Zamor, J. C. (ed.). 1985. *Public Participation in Development Planning and Management: Cases from Africa and Asia.* Boulder: Westview Press.

Gellner, E. 1981a. *Muslim Society.* London: Cambridge University Press.

Gellner, E. 1981b. The tribal society and its enemies. In Tapper, R. (ed.), *The Conflict of Tribe and State.* London: Croom Helm.

Gillespie, K. 1984. *Tripartite Relationship: Government, Foreign Investors, and Local Investors During Egypt's Economic Opening.* New York: Praeger.

Glisson, C. A., and Martin, P. Y. 1980. Productivity and efficiency in human service organizations as related to structure, size and age. *Academy of Management Journal 23(1)*, 21–3.

Gortner, H., Mahler, J., and Nicholson, J. 1986. *Organization Theory: A Public Perspective.* Homewood, Ill.: Dorsey.

Gregory, S. W., Jr. 1985. Auto traffic in Egypt as a verdant grammer. *Social Psychology Quarterly, 48(4)*, 337–48.

Gricar, B. G. 1981. *Making Organizations Humane and Productive.* New York: Wiley.

Grindle, M. (ed.). 1980. *Politics and Policy Implementation in the Third World.* Princeton: Princeton University.

Hage, J., and Finsterbusch, K. 1987. *Organizational Change as a Development Strategy* Boulder: Lynne Rienner Publishers.

Haire, M., Ghiselli, E. E., and Porter, L. W. 1966. *Managerial Thinking: An International Study.* New York: Wiley.

Hall, R. 1980. Effectiveness theory and organization effectiveness. *Journal of Applied Behavioral Science 16.*

Hall, R. 1982. *Organizations: Structure and Process,* 3rd ed. Englewood Cliffs, N.J.: Prentice-Hall.

Hamady, S. 1960. *Temperament and Character of the Arabs.* New York: Twayne Publishers.

Hammergren, S. L. 1983. *Development and the Politics of Administrative Reform: Lessons from Latin America.* Boulder: Westview Press.

Hansen, B., and Radway, S. 1982. *Employment Opportunities and Equity in Egypt.* Geneva: International Labor Office.

Harbison, F., and Ibrahim, I. A. 1958. *Human Resources for Egyptian Enterprise.* New York: McGraw-Hill.

Harmon, M. M. 1981. *Action Theory for Public Administration.* New York: Longman.

Harmon, M. M., and Mayer, R. T. 1986. *Organization Theory for Public Administration.* Boston: Little, Brown.

Heady, F. 1984. *Public Administration: A Comparative Perspective,* 3rd ed. New York: Marcel Dekker.

Henderson, K. M. 1983. *The Study of Public Administration*. Lanham, Md.: University Press of America.

Hersey, P., and Blanchard, K. 1982. *Management of Organizational Behavior*, 4th ed. Englewood Cliffs, N.J.: Prentice Hall.

Herzberg, F. 1976. *The Managerial Choice*. Homewood, Ill.: Dow Jones-Irwin.

Hofstede, G. 1984. *Culture's Consequences*. Beverly Hills: Sage.

Honadle, G. 1982a. Development administration in the eighties: New agendas or old perspectives? *Public Administration Review 42(2)*, 174–79.

Honadle, G. 1982b. Rapid reconnaissance for development administration: Mapping and moulding organizational landscapes. *World Development 10(8)*, 633–49.

Hopkins, N. S. 1987. *Agrarian Transformation in Egypt*. Boulder: Westview Press.

Hopwood, D. 1982. *Egypt: Politics and Society 1945–1981*. London: Allen and Unwin.

Horowitz, I. L. 1985–86. The 'Rashomon' effect: Ideological proclivities and political dilemmas of the IMF *Journal of Interamerican Studies 27(4)*.

Hunt, J., Hosking, D., Schriesheim, C., and Steward, R. 1984. *Leaders and Managers: International Perspectives on Managerial Behavior and Leadership*. New York: Pergamon.

Hyden, G. 1983. *No Shortcuts to Progress*. Berkeley: University of California Press.

Ibrahim, S. E. 1977. Toward a Sociological Theory for Development in the Third World (Arabic Text). Second Annual Scientific Conference for Egyptian Economists, Cairo, March.

Ingraham, P. W., and Barrilleau, C. 1983. Motivating government managers for retrenchment: Some possible lessons from the senior executive service. *Public Administration Review, 43(3)*, 393–402.

Inkeles, A., and Smith, D. 1974. *Becoming Modern*. Cambridge: Harvard University Press.

Jun, J. 1976. Renewing the study of comparative administration: Some reflections on the current possibilities. *Public Administration 36(6)*, 641–47.

Kanter, R., and Brinkerhoff, D. 1981. Organizational performance: Recent developments in measurement. *Annual Review of Sociology 7*, 321–49.

Kast, F. E., and Rosenzweig, J. E. 1981. *Organization and Management: A Systems and Contingency Approach*, 3rd ed. London: McGraw-Hill.

Kats, G. 1983. The population factor. *Cairo Today*, January, 26–44.

Katz, D., and Kahn, R. 1978. *The Social Psychology of Organizations*. New York: Wiley.

Kent, T., and McAllister, I. 1985. *Management for Development: Planning and Practice from African and Canadian Experience*. Lanham, Md.: University Press of America.

Kerrigan, J. E., and Luke, J. S. 1987. *Management Training Strategies for Developing Countries.* Boulder: Lynne Rienner.

Khuri, F I. (ed.). 1981. *Leadership and Development in Arab Society.* Syracuse: Syracuse University Press.

Kiggundu, M. N., Jorgensen, J. J., and Hafsi, T. 1983. Administrative theory and practice in developing countries: A synthesis. *Administrative Science Quarterly 28(1),* 66–83.

Kirk-Greene, A. 1984. *Studies in African Administration.* London: Frank Cass.

Kirkpatrick, C. H., Lee, N., and Nixson, F 1984. *Industrial Structure and Policy in Less Developed Countries.* Winchester, Mass.: Allen & Unwin.

Kopec, A. 1985. USAID in Egypt: An interview with Frank Kimball, Director of USAID in Egypt. *Cairo Today,* November.

Krauss, M. B. 1984. *Development Without Aid: Growth, Poverty and Government.* Lanham, Md.: University Press of America.

Lane, E. W. 1908. *Manners and Customs of the Modern Egyptians.* London: J. M. Dent & Sons.

LaPalombara, J. (ed.). 1963. *Bureaucracy and Political Development.* Princeton: Princeton University Press.

Lerner, A. W. 1986. Ambiguity and organizational analysis: The consequences of micro versus macro conceptualization. *Administration and Society, 17(4),* 461–79.

Lerner, D. 1958. *The Passing of Traditional Societies.* Glenco, Ill.: Free Press.

Likert, R. 1958. Measuring organizational performance. *Harvard Business Review 36(2),* 41–51.

Lindenberg, M., and Crosby, B. 1981. *Managing Development: The Political Dimension.* Hartford: Kumarian.

Livingstone, H., and Wilkie, R. 1981. Motivation and performance among civil service managers. *Public Administration, 59(Summer),* 151–73.

Lutfi, A. 1985. Ten economic causes. Trans. M. Palmer. Cairo: *Al Ahram Iktisadi 869* (September 9).

Luke, D. F 1986. Trends in development administration: The continuing challenge to the efficacy of the post-colonial state in the Third World. *Public Administration and Development 6(1),* 73–85.

MacPherson, S. 1982. *Social Policy in the Third World: The Social Dilemmas of Underdevelopment.* Titiwa, N.J.: Rowman and Littlefield.

Mahran, M. 1984. In the control center: An investigation. *Al Mussawar* (Cairo Arabic Weekly). June 8.

McClelland, D. C. 1961. *The Achieving Society.* Princeton: Van Nostrand.

Mendoza, G. A. 1977. The transferability of Western management concepts and programs: An Asian perspective. In J. E. Black, J. S. Coleman, and L. D. Stifel (eds.), *Education and Training for Public Sector Management in Developing Countries.* New York: Rockefeller Foundation, 61–71.

Miller, T. C. 1984. *Public Sector Performance: A Conceptual Turning Point.* Baltimore: Johns Hopkins.

Montgomery, J. D. 1985. *The African Manager.* Washington, D.C.: National Association of Schools of Public Affairs and Administration.

Montgomery, J. D., and Siffin, W. (eds.). 1966. *Approaches to Development: Politics, Administration and Change.* New York: McGraw-Hill.

Mubarak, Hosni (President). 1985. Address to the Egyptian Parliament. *Al Ahram,* November 14.

Mubarak, Hosni (President). 1983. Presentation before the Economic Conference: February 13, 1982. *Speeches and Discussions of President Hosni Mubarak: January 1982–July 1982.* Cairo: Ministry of Information.

Muna, F. 1981. *The Arab Executive.* London: Macmillan.

Murelius, O. 1981. *An Institutional Approach to Project Analysis in Developing Countries.* Washington, D.C.: OECD Publications.

Nachmias, D., and Rosenbloom, D. H. 1978. *Bureaucratic Culture.* New York: St. Martin's Press.

Neff, W. S. 1985. *Work and Human Behavior,* 3rd ed. Hawthorne, N.Y.: Aldine de Gruyter.

Nevis, E. C. 1984. Using an American perspective in understanding another culture: Toward a hierarchy of needs for the People's Republic of China. *Journal of Applied Behavioral Science, 19(4).*

Nigro, L. G. 1984. *Decision Making in the Public Sector.* New York: Marcel Dekker.

Nyrop, R. F 1983. *Egypt: A Country Study.* Washington, D.C.: Foreign Area Studies, The American University.

Omer, S. M. 1983. *Institution Building and Comprehensive Social Development.* Lanham, Md.: University Press of America.

Peters, G. 1984. *The Politics of Bureaucracy.* New York: Longman.

Puthucheavy, M. 1978. *The Politics of Administration: The Malaysian Experience.* London: Oxford University Press.

Rainey, H. G. 1983. Public organization theory: The rising challenge. *Public Administration Review 43(2),* 176–82.

Riggs, F W. (ed.). 1970. *Frontiers of Development Administration.* Durham, N.C.: Duke University Press.

Roy, R. H. 1977. *The Culture of Management.* Baltimore: Johns Hopkins University Press.

Selim, L. 1976. In search of comparative administration. *Public Administration Review 36(6),* 621–25.

Silveira, M. P. (ed.). 1985. *Research and Development.* Boulder: Westview Press.

Smith, P. M. 1986. *Taking Charge.* Washington, D.C.: National Defense University Press.

Spicer, M. W. 1985. A public choice approach to motivating people in bureaucratic organizations. *Academy of Management Review 10(3)*, 518–26.

Suleiman, E. N. 1985. *Bureaucrats and Policy Making: A Comparative Overview.* New York: Holmes & Meier.

Sullivan, E. L. 1986. *Women in Egyptian Public Life.* Syracuse: Syracuse University Press.

Tapper, R. (ed.). 1983. *The Conflict of Tribe and State.* London: Croom Helm.

Taylor, J. G. 1979. *From Modernization to Modes of Production: A Critique of the Sociologies of Development and Underdevelopment.* Atlantic Highlands, N.J.: Humanities Press.

Tessler, M., Palmer, M., Farfah, T., and Ibrahim, B. 1987. *The Evaluation and Application of Survey Research in the Arab World.* Boulder: Westview Press.

Thompson, V. A. 1969. *Bureaucracy and Innovation.* Tuscaloosa, Ala.: University of Alabama Press.

Tulchin, J. S. 1985. *Habitat, Health, and Developments: A New Way of Looking at Cities in the Third World.* Boulder: Lynne Rienner.

Tummala, K. K. (ed.). 1984. *Administrative Systems Abroad,* rev. ed., Lanham, Md.: University Press of America.

Waldo, D. 1964. *Comparative Public Administration: Prologue, Problems, and Promise.* Chicago: Comparative Public Administration Group, American Society for Public Administration.

Waterbury, J. 1978. *Egypt, Burdens of the Past: Options for the Future.* Bloomington, Ind.: Indiana University Press.

Waterbury, J. 1979. *Hydropolitics of the Nile Valley.* Syracuse: Syracuse University Press.

Waterbury, J. 1983. *The Egypt of Nasser and Sadat: The Political Economy of Two Regimes.* Princeton: Princeton University Press.

Weber, M. 1947. *The Theory of Social and Economic Organization.* New York: Macmillan.

Weick, K. E. 1979. *The Social Psychology of Organizing,* 2nd ed. Reading, Mass.: Addison-Wesley.

Weinbaum, M. G. 1986. *Egypt and the Politics of U.S. Economic Aid.* Boulder, Colo.: Westview Press.

Weinbaum, M. G., and Naim, R. 1983. Domestic and International Politics in Egypt's Economic Policy Reforms. Paper presented at the Convention of the Middle East Studies Association of North America, Chicago, November.

White, L. G. 1987. *Creating Opportunities for Change: Approaches to Managing Development Programs.* Boulder, Colo.: Lynne Rienner.

Wholey, J. S., Abramson, M. A., and Bellavita, C. 1986. *Performance and Credibility.* Lexington, Mass.: Lexington Books.

Youssef, H. 1982. *The Palace: Its Role in Egyptian Politics* (Arabic text). Cairo: Al Ahram.

Youssef, S. M. 1983. *System of Management in Egyptian Public Enterprises.* Cairo: Center for Middle East Management Studies, The American University in Cairo.

Yukl, G. A. 1981. *Leadership in Organizations.* Englewood Cliffs, N.J.: Prentice-Hall.

Zaki, R. 1983. *The Egyptian Economic Crisis* (Arabic text). Cairo: Library Madbouli.

Index

Absenteeism in government service, 14
Achievement values, 31, 100. *See also* Values
Administrators, 21
Age, effect of, 131–32, 145, 153, 154, 156
Agriculture, need for improvements in, 11, 15
Aid, foreign, 12, 13–15. *See also* USAID
Al Ahram Center for Strategic and Political Studies, ix–x, 1; questionnaire of 42–44, 171 n.7 (chap. 7)
Ali, Mohammed, 27–28
Aluminum Corporation, x, 42, 48, 145–46, 153, 163; bureaucratic capacity of, 123–26; communication at, 125, 126, 146; morale of, 146; peer evaluations of, 126; rural location of, 65, 161; *wasta* and, 125
Apathy, 14, 15, 23, 31, 38, 45, 114; authority and, 76; explanations of, 59–63, 101–4; job satisfaction and, 33; low productivity and, 46; peer evaluations of, 55, 56; status deprivation and, 111
Arab Socialist Union, 6
Arab unity, Nasser's quest for, 5
Authority, 37; concentration of, 75–86, 89, 90, 99, 101, 104, 117, 124, 131, 149, 156, 158; delegation of, 32, 78, 122, 124–25, 128, 149; hierarchies, 20, 23; inadequate, 99, 144; reluctance to delegate, 82, 83, 101, 104, 153, 156; respect for, 34–35; tables, 50, 79, 81, 103, 143; *wasta* and, 76, 80

Ayubi, Nazih M. (cited), ix, 22, 36, 38, 43, 80, 86, 147

Banking, private sector and, 6, 15
Behavioral capacity. *See* Bureaucratic behavior; Bureaucratic capacity
Berger, Morroe (cited), 36, 43
Bureaucratic appointments, 25–26
Bureaucratic behavior, 20, 33–37, 114, 147–64; attributes of, 30–33, 121–46; bureaucratic flexibility and, 75–90; relationship between sex and, 132–33,
Bureaucratic capacity, 1, 19–20, 121–64; age and, 131–32; education and, 126–29; group dynamics and, 138–40, 156; job level and, 129–31; job unit and, 123–26; media preferences and, 133–38; sex and, 132–33; supervisor dynamics and, 140–42; systemic variables and, 142–44
Bureaucratic careers, 38; 39
Bureaucratic culture, 33–41, 154, 156
Bureaucratic expansion, 4, 5, 8, 37–38
Bureaucratic flexibility, 32, 73–90, 131, 149–50, 154; authority and, 75–81, 158; communication and, 86–89, 158; culture and, 129, 145, 156; education and, 128; group dynamics scale and, 122; job level and, 130; job unit and, 124; media preferences and, 133; responsibility and, 82–86; table, 50

183

Bureaucratic performance. *See* Bureaucratic behavior
Bureaucratic reform, 15–18, 152–53, 158, 159, 162, 164
Bureaucratic status, 120, 132, 136; morale and, 111; table, 112
Bureaucratic structure, 19–23, 41, 46, 75, 98–101, 158–59

Cairo, 12, 65, 73–74, 115, 126, 161
Capitalism under Sadat, 95
Centralization. *See* Authority, concentration of
Change, organizational, 56
Communication, 20, 32, 33, 113, 140–42, 158; Aluminum Corporation and, 125, 126, 146; between bureaucracy and public, 115, 117; bureaucratic flexibility and, 86–89, 158; tables, 87, 88, 116
Competitiveness, 98–99
Construction industry, 6, 15, 46
Corruption, 30, 33, 159, 167 n. 15
Cotton, 3, 12–13
Cultural values, 128, 129, 136, 152, 155, 160; tables, 60, 103. *See also* Values
Culture, 100–104; Egyptian, 37, 40, 80, 138, 145, 154, 158, 162; table, 103
Currency, 12, 16

Data processing equipment, 22
Decentralization, 21, 126
Decision making, 91, 94, 96–97, 124, 153; innovation and, 104–6, 128–32, 137–38, 145, 150, 154, 156, 160, 162; innovation scale and, 97, 122, 130, 140; tables, 79, 96, 139
Defection from bureaucracy, 23, 24, 62
Demographics, 125–26

Economics, 45–46, 95, 119; problems, 2–3, 6–7, 12–13, 17, 23–24, 55, 107–8; table, 94

Education, x, 136; bureaucratic capacity and, 126–29; Egyptian, 4, 13, 28; innovation and, 128, 129; productivity and, 127, 145, 153, 154, 160; table, 143
Egypt: economic and social development of, ix, 1–7, 14–18, 147, 157; historical traditions of, 37, 78, 80; problems in, 2, 11–14, 73, 108, 150; rulers of, 37
Egyptian-Israeli relations, 5, 6
Employment: full, 7, 47, 59, 78; government, 8; supplementary, 23, 24, 41, 47, 61–62, 67, 69, 70, 142, 144, 154–55. *See also* Unemployment
Evaluation procedures, 22, 25, 33, 109–10, 148, 161. *See also* Peer evaluations
Exports, 3, 12, 23

Family: bonds, 89; patterns in, 37, 155; proximity to, 64, 67, 125; tables, 66–67, 88, 139
Fellahin, 11
Farouk I, 3, 4
Fatalism in Egyptian society, 100
Favoritism, 30, 33, 34, 167 n. 15; table, 63
Female workers. *See* Workers, female
Flexibility. *See* Bureaucratic flexibility
Ford Foundation, ix, 1
Foreign relations, 6
Full employment. *See* Employment, full

Garyah administrators. *See* Administrators
Graduates policy, 4–5, 28–29, 41, 47, 60, 125, 158, 166 n. 13; problems with, 8, 15, 16, 22; table, 40; as welfare system, 25, 38, 98; women and, 133
Great Britain, 3, 28, 69; job satisfaction in, 57, 149
Group dynamics, 101, 102, 104, 138–40, 152, 153, 156; tables, 60, 103
Group dynamics scale: bureaucratic attitudes toward public and, 109–10; bureaucratic capacity and, 138–40, 156; bureaucratic flexibility and, 122; inno-

vation and, 92–94; productivity and, 48–50, 55; responsibility avoidance and, 83; table, 50

Herzberg, Frederick, 33, 54, 57–59, 67–69, 99, 142, 149, 169 n. 8; table, 52–53

Ibrahim, Saad Eddin (cited), 40
Imports, Egyptian dependency upon, 15, 23, 24
Incentives, 15, 20, 23, 27, 45–48, 59, 102, 126, 149, 160, 168 n. 5; cross-cultural data and, 68–69; monetary, 23, 46–47, 63–65, 68, 70–71, 149, 160, 162; morale and, 47; tables, 60, 63, 103. See also Monetary values; Prestige
Incentive values. See Motivational values
Infitah (open-door policy), 6, 7, 11, 24, 26, 41, 46, 61, 157
Inflation, 23–24
Influence. See Wasta
Information: professional, 49, 122; quality of, 22, 86, 144; sources of, 138, 168 n. 6; tables, 139, 143
Innovation, 31, 34, 91–106, 122, 132, 150, 159, 161–62; education and, 128, 129; group dynamics scale and, 92–94; job level and, 130–31; job unit and, 124; media preference and, 133; peer evaluations of, 92; social, 94, 95, 104–5, 128, 129, 131, 145, 150, 154, 156; tables, 93, 94, 96, 103. See also Decision making, innovation and
Insecurity, and as aspect of bureaucratic behavior, 103, 104, 155
International Monetary Fund, 11, 16, 17, 24, 41
Islam, influence of, 6, 95
Israel. See Egyptian-Israeli relations

Job comfort, 51, 56, 64, 67, 122, 169 n. 7; table, 66–67

Job dissatisfaction, 54, 57, 65, 67, 68; table, 52–53
Job level, 130–31, 154, 156
Job location, 64, 65, 67, 125, 126, 146, 155, 161; table, 66–67
Job satisfaction, 33, 54, 57–59; cross-national data, 57–58; productivity and, 121–22, 123, 127, 130, 138, 144, 148–49; among Saudi bureaucrats, 69; tables, 51, 52–53
Job security, 35–36, 41, 47, 51, 54, 61, 64, 155, 169 n. 7; tables, 50, 66–67, 103
June war of 1967, 26

Kimball, Frank (cited), 7–8

Labor force, 12
Livingstone, Hugh (cited), 57, 69
Loyalty, political, 26, 40
Lutfi, Ali (cited), 107–8, 119

Male workers. See Workers, male
Management, theories of, 47, 89
Markaz administrators. See Administrators
Mass employment. See Employment, full
Media, influence of, 133–38, 145, 154; tables, 134–36, 139
Merit examinations, 38, 60–61
Migration, 11, 12, 70, 133
Military, as source for filling bureaucratic positions 5, 40
Ministries, government, 20, 21, 27, 38
Ministry of Industry, x, 42, 48, 123–26, 145, 153
Ministry of Labor, 38
Ministry of Local Government, 21
Ministry of Social Affairs, x, 42, 123–26, 145, 153
Monarchy, effects of, 3, 4, 28, 75, 111, 114
Monetary values, 64–65, 68, 69, 122, 155. See also Values

Morale, 24, 29, 104, 120, 125, 126, 161;
  Aluminum Corporation, 146; bureaucratic status and, 111; incentives
  and, 47; job satisfaction and, 33; salaries and, 8–9, 23, 41, 62
Motivational values, 63–71, 125–26, 149,
  155, 160, 163, 169 n. 7; psychological,
  68–69, 152; table, 66–67. *See also*
  Values
Mubarak, Hosni, 10–18, 29, 33–34, 95;
  on apathy, 45; on bureaucracy and the
  public, 107, 110, 158; on economic
  growth, 22; on incentives, 46, 63; on
  productivity, 55; on public sector, 27;
  on salaries, 24
Muna, Farid A. (cited), 43

Nasser, Abdul, 2–10, 16, 28, 29; bu-
  reaucracy under, 4–5, 20, 25, 26, 38,
  75, 114; economy under, 9, 61, 95; on
  public sector, 39
National Democratic Party, 18
Nationalization policies, 3, 4, 20, 40
Nepotism, 33, 167 n. 15
Nevis, E. C. (cited), 68
Nigeria, civil servants in, 68
Nyrop, Richard (cited), 20–21

Oil, economic importance of, 12, 13, 14,
  24
Open-door policy. *See Infitah*
Outside employment. *See* Employment,
  supplementary
Overstaffing. *See* Staffing, overstaffing

Peer evaluations, 58, 119, 140, 155, 156;
  Aluminum Corporation, 126; of ac-
  ceptance of responsibility, 124; of apathy, 55, 56; of bureaucratic attitudes
  toward the public, 109–10; of innovation, 92; of productivity, 122, 127
Persian Gulf, economic opportunities in,

9, 23, 62, 67
Pharaohs, 37
Politics, 6, 18, 24–27
Population, growth of, 1, 2, 3, 11, 12,
  14, 108
Prestige, importance of in Egyptian society, 47, 64–71, 112, 122, 126, 149,
  155, 160; tables, 39, 66–67
Price controls, 11, 15
Price supports, 6, 11, 12, 16–17, 24, 46,
  108
Private sector, 6, 8, 9, 22, 24, 46, 62, 133;
  and public sector, 17, 25, 27, 61, 98,
  157, 163, 172 n. 1; role in economic
  development, 7, 15, 157, 163; salaries,
  23, 29, 40, 46–47, 61, 70, 98
Productivity, 23, 33, 34, 35, 45–71, 123–
  46, 148–49, 153–64; education and,
  127, 145, 153, 154, 160; evaluation of,
  48, 55, 148; group dynamics scale and,
  48–50, 55; job satisfaction and, 121–22,
  123, 129, 130, 138, 144, 148–49; low,
  14, 45, 46, 55, 60, 149, 153; measures
  of, 48–59, 121–23; morale and, 126;
  peer evaluations of, 122, 127; positive
  reinforcement and, 140–42; tables, 49,
  51, 60, 63; training and, 127–29
Professional-reference indicator, 49, 56–
  57, 58, 122, 123, 127, 130, 137–38,
  144; table, 51; women and, 133
Promotion, bureaucratic, 20, 125, 126,
  132, 146, 153, 162
Public: bureaucratic attitudes toward, 36,
  107–20, 122–23, 128–29, 131, 133, 140,
  144, 145, 150–51, 154, 156, 159, 163;
  confidence in bureaucracy, 33, 34, 107,
  112; government and, 22, 73; interaction with bureaucracy, 27–30, 32, 33,
  76, 107–20, 128–29, 150–51, 163; relationship with political elite, 29, 114;
  tables, 50, 112, 113, 116, 119; *wasta*
  and, 108, 112, 113, 117, 119, 151
Public administration, 30, 138, 152
Public sector, 7, 8, 39; corporations, 4, 6,
  7, 15, 20–21, 26, 27, 34, 38, 40, 46,
  123; and private sector, 17, 25, 61, 98,
  157, 163, 172 n. 1; salaries, 29, 46, 61,
  98

Real estate, private interests in, 6, 15, 46
Recruitment, 20, 22, 33, 38, 59–61, 125, 144, 146, 161, 162; tables, 40, 63; welfare-oriented, 98, 99, 161
Reinforcement, positive, among bureaucrats, 141–42, 156–57
Red tape, 15, 21–22, 32, 62, 76, 114–15, 118; tables, 63, 85
Relatives. See Family
Religion, 144, 171 n. 7
Research, survey, 43, 168 n. 27
Responsibility: assumption of, 23, 32, 82, 103, 122, 124, 128, 140, 158; avoidance of, 77, 80–81, 82–86, 90, 117, 149–50; peer evaluations of, 124; poorly defined, 46, 55, 99; tables, 39, 50, 60, 66–67, 81, 85, 103
Revolution of 1952, 3, 28, 40, 158
Rigidity. See Bureaucratic flexibility
Risk taking, need for, 31, 34, 77, 99, 122, 124; tables, 50, 66–67, 103

Sadat, Anwar; 2–10, 16, 80; bureaucracy under, 8–9, 20, 21, 26, 38, 114; economy under, 9, 11, 16, 46, 61, 95; public interaction with bureaucracy under, 29, 108
Salaries, 8–9, 20, 29, 54, 68–70; government, 8, 17, 22–25, 41, 46–47, 55, 61–71, 85, 98–99, 155; incentives and, 46; increases in, 65, 152–53, 159, 160; job dissatisfaction and, 57, 65; morale and, 8–9, 23, 41, 62; private sector, 23, 29, 40, 46–47, 61, 70, 98; public sector, 29, 46, 61, 98; tables, 52–53, 63, 66–67
Second Jobs. See Employment: supplementary
Self-esteem, in Middle Eastern societies, 100
Skill, levels of, 102, 153, 154; low, 22, 80, 82, 98, 101, 126–27, 131, 144; tables, 60, 63, 81, 103
Social innovation. See Innovation, social
Socialism: economic and welfare policies of, 24; as Egyptian ideology, 4, 6, 26, 28–29, 39, 95; government regulation

under, 61; laws of 1961 and, 20
Social values, 94–95, 100, 138. See also Values
Soviet Union, influence of, 6, 123
Staffing, 20, 86, 98; overstaffing, 22, 23, 25, 46, 98
Stimuli, hygienic and motivational, 54, 68, 69, 142
Supervisor dynamics, 101, 102, 104, 140–42, 152, 153, 156–57; and positive reinforcement, 140–42, 156–57; tables, 52–53, 60, 63, 85, 87, 88, 96, 103, 139, 141
Supplementary employment. See Employment, supplementary
Survey research. See Research, survey

Tourism, economic value of, 6, 12, 15, 18, 46
Trade: deficit, 45; exports, 3, 12, 23; imbalance, 14; imports, 15, 23, 24
Training, 20, 121, 125, 145, 154, 160, 162; productivity and, 127–29; tables, 79, 143
Turnover, 33, 62

Unemployment, 16, 17
United States: Egyptian allegiance to, 6; policy of toward price supports, 11, 16; results of surveys in, 68, 69, 70
USAID, 6–8, 13, 15, 24, 37, 41

Value-based indicators, 122, 138; table, 51
Values, 47, 63–65, 68, 95, 100, 122, 126, 128, 133, 158. See also Achievement values; Cultural values; Monetary values; Motivational values; Social values

Wages. See Salaries
Wasta (influence), use of, 26, 33, 38, 55,

60–61, 89, 157; Aluminum Corpora-
tion and, 125; authority and, 76, 80;
public and, 108, 112, 113, 117, 119,
151; table, 40
Waterbury, John (cited), 172 n. 1
Weber, Max (cited), 39
Welfare system: bureaucracy as, 16, 25,
38, 98, 158
Wilkie, Roy (cited), 57, 69
Women. *See* Workers, female
Work ethic, 100
Working conditions, 22, 23, 54; table,
52–53
Work-value indicator, 49, 56, 58–59, 122,

130, 161–62, 163, 169 n. 7, 171 n. 7;
table, 51; women and, 133
Workers: female, 64–65, 133; male, 64,
125, 133

Youssef, Hassan (cited), 165 n. 1
Youssef, Samir M. (cited), ix, 22, 26, 39,
40, 43, 147

Zaki, Ramzi (cited), 22

THE EGYPTIAN BUREAUCRACY

was composed in 10½ on 12 Bembo on a Linotron 202
by Coghill Book Typesetting Co.;
with display type set in Friz Quadrata
by Dix Type, Inc.
printed by sheet-fed offset on 50-pound, acid-free Glatfelter Natural Hi Bulk,
Smyth-sewn and bound over binder's boards in Joanna Arrestox B,
with dust jackets printed in two colors,
by Braun-Brumfield, Inc.;
and published by

SYRACUSE UNIVERSITY PRESS
Syracuse, New York 13244-5160